1988

Also by Paul Goldberger
The City Observed: New York

THE SKYSCRAPER

THE SKYSCRAPER

PAUL GOLDBERGER

ALFRED A. KNOPF
NEW YORK 1986

For Susan
and for Adam

This is a Borzoi Book
Published by Alfred A. Knopf, Inc.

Library of Congress Cataloging in Publication Data

Goldberger, Paul
    The skyscraper.

    1. Skyscrapers—United States   I. Title.
NA6230.G59 1981   725'.23'0973   81-47480
ISBN 0-394-50595-6   AACR2
ISBN 0-394-71586-1 (pbk.)

Manufactured in the United States of America
Published November 24, 1981
Reprinted Twice
Fourth Printing, September 1986

 Created by Media Projects, Inc.

Contents

ACKNOWLEDGMENTS

No book is fully the work of one person, and a book that makes much use of photographs tends particularly to require outside assistance. This book is no exception, and it is a pleasure to acknowledge here those who have been of help. Carter Smith first conceived this project, and his staff at Media Projects, Inc., led by Sarah Jones and Ellen Coffey, did the major work of gathering photographs. Ann Close not only edited the text, but graciously allowed herself to be conscripted into the efforts of picture research; I am especially grateful for her constant good humor throughout. The process of gathering photographs brought the picture researchers into contact with a number of people and institutions which were unusually giving of their time and expertise: among them were Richard Whittingham, Cervin Robinson, Ezra Stoller, David Dunlap, Richard Wurts of Wurts Brothers, the Museum of the City of New York, The Chicago Historical Society, Rockefeller Center, and the Library of Congress. The chance to use the splendid archival photographs of Irving Underhill and of Wurts Brothers is a special privilege.

I owe other debts. Some go back in time: to Vincent Scully, whose own rethinking of the role of eclecticism in skyscraper design has affected my own; to the students of the Yale School of Architecture, whose studio on skyscraper design under Cesar Pelli in 1979 helped clarify my own ideas. More recently, Christopher Gray of the Office for Metropolitan History provided skillful and efficient research assistance; Vance Freymann and Jonnel Raab typed sections of the manuscript with dispatch. Peter Katz of Whitehouse & Katz joined the project late and brought it to a surprisingly smooth conclusion with his design; this project could not have taken its present form without his considerable skills. I must again thank Ann Close for orchestrating the many parts of this project so well. And as I worked, my wife Susan and my son Adam offered the most precious gift, impatience.

Paul Goldberger

New York, June 1981

PREFACE

This is a history and commentary on the greatest of American building forms, the skyscraper. But it is commentary more than it is history, since there seems little need to duplicate the already excellent scholarship that exists on the beginnings of the skyscraper in the nineteenth century and on the great monuments created in the twentieth. Where this book differs most from what has been written before is in emphasis—I am attracted to the flamboyant, eclectic skyscrapers inspired by the theatrical impulses of New York as much as, if not more than, I am to the more intellectually rigorous skyscrapers of Chicago, and thus these buildings get a substantial share of attention. My hope, however, is not to praise the stage sets of the 1920's at the expense of the glass boxes of the 1950's, or to set the traditions of one city against those of another, but rather to put all phases of skyscraper development together into a single narrative. It is all one story, from Louis Sullivan's earnest search for a new skyscraper style in Chicago in the 1890's to Philip Johnson and John Burgee's startling use of classical forms in towers for the 1980's.

The focus here is on American skyscrapers. There is no nationalistic bias intended—it is simply that the most significant or interesting skyscrapers have been designed by American architects and built on American soil. As a history of the twentieth-century musical theater would be primarily a history of the American musical comedy, so do skyscrapers seem to be a form born and developed best on this continent. There are a few important skyscrapers by American architects that have been built abroad—I. M. Pei's Oversea Chinese Bank tower in Singapore is perhaps the finest recent example—but these are the rare exceptions. As for works of non-Americans, even the better examples, such as Gio Ponti's Pirelli headquarters in Milan, or the recent and inventive group of Japanese towers, seem to play only a peripheral role in the development of the skyscraper form. And most other non-American skyscrapers, such as the Maine-Montparnasse tower and the buildings of La Défense in Paris, are merely mediocre imitations of American postwar structures. That these American towers came in part from theoretical models developed by Europeans is important, not to mention ironic, but it does little to spark real interest in the new European buildings themselves.

The concerns here are primarily esthetic ones. The development of the technology of the skyscraper has been described sufficiently elsewhere, although of course that technology continues to evolve. For such buildings as the World Trade Center in New York, the Sears Tower in Chicago, and the American Telephone and Telegraph Building under construction in New York, the work of the engineers has been as creative as that of the architects who conceived the buildings' basic forms, if not more so. The engineering aspects of skyscrapers will be referred to, but not discussed in detail, though it should be mentioned here that the current trend toward more varied shapes has required of the engineering profession considerable effort, and structural engineers have not flinched at the challenge of finding a way to give physical reality to almost any form architects have invented in the past few years.

The subject of planning is another one that cannot be fully separated from the esthetics of the skyscraper: without coherent planning, the finest urban skyscrapers imaginable will have little value. There were cries that cities were becoming overbuilt as early as the turn of the century, and these complaints are discussed in the first chapter; the debate was renewed in the 1920's, as Chapter Five will explain. Approval of skyscrapers often became a way of judging approval of the city itself. Frank Lloyd Wright, a notorious opponent of the traditional, dense city, argued that skyscrapers should be built in the country if at all. In later years Lewis Mumford wrote with particular eloquence of the dangers of cramming too many buildings into too small a space: "If [midtown Manhattan] ceases to be a milieu in which people can exist in reasonable contentment instead of as prisoners perpetually plotting to escape a concentration camp, it will be unprofitable to discuss architectural achievements—buildings that occasionally cause people to hold their breath for a stabbing moment or that restore them to equilibrium by offering them a prospect of space and form joyfully mastered."

Mumford's warning, published in an essay entitled "The Two-Way Flood" in *The New Yorker* in 1955, may have been premature then. But it speaks with urgency to us today, when several American cities are again in the midst of vast construction. Manhattan, in particular, is being built to a density that begins to defy common sense. It seems to me that one can appreciate, even prefer, the congested aspect of urban life and still admit that there are limits to density, and that we may finally, a quarter-century after Mumford proclaimed the danger, be approaching them.

In the East Fifties at Madison Avenue, three vast skyscrapers are rising within the space of two city blocks, and several others are going up nearby. As of this writing there is barely a site available for building in that neighborhood—and even St. Bartholomew's Church, the Bertram Goodhue-designed landmark of 1919, is considering the sale of its adjacent community house and its replacement with a high tower on Park Avenue's only remaining open space. Even the church, it would seem, is not immune to the current pressure to fill every inch of ground and sky.

Ironically, almost all of the new New York towers are by architects of some renown, and the complaint that was so valid in the 1960's—that only commercial architects of little imagination were given commissions to build large-scale, center-city towers—is no longer true. But whatever the serious architectural intent of any new construction, in New York and elsewhere, it may not matter very much if the insistence upon forcing one 50-story tower next to another continues much longer.

THE SKYSCRAPER

CHAPTER ONE

THE SKYSCRAPER VS. THE CITY

Aside from all the aesthetic considerations the continued erection of the so-called "skyscraper," the excessively tall building, constitutes a menace to public health and safety and an offence which must be stopped. —David Knickerbocker Boyd, *American Architect and Building News,* November 18, 1908

Behind the skyscraper stand the leading parts of the nation. . . . Those who advocate its abolition will certainly have no success. —Francisco Mujica, *History of the Skyscraper,* 1929

The skyscraper is at once the triumphant symbol of and the unwelcome intruder in the American city. We seem, after nearly a century, still not fully at peace with tall buildings: they shatter scale and steal light, and it is no surprise to hear them denounced as monstrous constructions; yet we also hold them dear—what brownstone has ever been the symbol of New York that the Empire State Building is, what lakefront park the icon of Chicago that the Sears Tower has become? To visitors and natives alike, these buildings *are* these cities; as Notre Dame does in Paris or the Houses of Parliament do in London, these skyscrapers seem not merely to suggest the personalities of the cities of which they are a part, but to have made these personalities—to have made these cities' characters reflections of their own qualities as objects.

Surely more than any other type of building the skyscraper is both quintessentially American and quintessentially of the twentieth century. It emerged in the nineteenth century and owes a certain debt to European architecture, but it was in the United States in the first four decades of this century that the skyscraper became not a curiosity of commercial architecture but a bold force, a force as powerful in its ability to transform the urban environment in its time as the automobile was to be in the decades succeeding. The notion of height was to become the overriding image of New York City in the years after 1900, and thus, by extension, the image of all American cities growing to maturity. The idea that a city is primarily an agglomeration of small- to medium-sized buildings, made urban by their closeness, was pushed aside by the coming of the skyscraper, and Americans began to define urbanity on the ba-

Opposite: "King's Dream of New York," by Harry M. Pettit. From King's Views of New York, *1908–09.*

3

Lower Broadway in New York, c. 1880. The portico of St. Paul's Chapel (Thomas McBean, 1766) is visible in the foreground; the spire of Trinity Church (Richard Upjohn, 1846) in the background. In the middle is the Western Union Building (George B. Post, 1875)—at 230 feet not as tall as Trinity's 284-foot spire.

sis of size. A city showed its might by how many buildings it had and how many people were in it, and, more to the point, by how big these buildings could be made to be. Our very notion of what cities were was changed forever.

It was thus that the skyscraper came to mean very different things to the twentieth century than it had to the nineteenth. The skyscrapers of the 1880's and 1890's were buildings that fit reasonably, if not fully, into the existing urban context; the newness of most of them lay in their technology rather than in their size or their style, and they did not appear to shatter their age's sense of what a city—or, indeed, what a building—was. They were taller than what had come before, but they were not tall enough to rule the skyline. If anything in their day grew really tall it was churches: the 200-foot steeple of St. Paul's Chapel on lower Broadway in New York was once the tallest building in the city; later that mantle would pass to the 284-foot Trinity Church, completed in 1846, and it would not be until 1892 that a secular building—George B. Post's Pulitzer Building on Park Row, 309 feet tall—would become the tallest building in New York.

So at the turn of the century there was still a fairly traditional sense of what a city was supposed to be. The vaunted ambition of a nation moving to fill a continent and eager to play a major role in the international balance of power was the force that most influenced architecture in terms of style; it helped create the surge of interest in classicism—the imperialist leanings of the Beaux-Arts being a perfect reflection of the nation's new self-image—and thus came a generation of railroad stations, museums, and other structures that bespoke a commitment to civic grandeur. But the notion of how cities and buildings should look was not fundamentally altered, and indeed, commercial architecture was affected only slightly. Business buildings had grown with the advent of the steel frame and the elevator, the two technological innovations that made great skyscrapers on the one hand possible and on the other hand practical, but they tended to be little more than 12 or 15 stories in height.

Even slightly larger buildings, like the St. Paul Building on Broadway and Ann Streets in New York or, a few blocks downtown, the 19-story American Surety Building at 100 Broadway, designed by Bruce Price and completed in 1894, tended to be flanked by smaller structures, so the general sense of scale to the passer-by was not dramatically different from what it had been. Five-, six-, seven-, and eight-story buildings lined the streets of commercial neighborhoods in New York, Philadelphia, Boston, and Chicago; there was a crowded sense of jostling to them, but it was energizing, not overpowering. Natural light was still a commodity that office workers and pedestrians alike expected, and some breadth of sky was not a vista that one had to travel out of the city to enjoy; nearly every corner offered some sense of openness, even if the view upward was punctuated by an elaborate mansard or a richly detailed cornice hung a hundred feet above the street.

It was into such a world, possessed of the technological achievements of the skyscraper but as yet unchanged by them, that the new generation of twentieth-century skyscrapers arrived. In 1906 plans were announced for the Singer Building in lower Manhattan, 600 feet of ornate brick and terra cotta that would be, the *New York Times* proclaimed at the top of page 1, "higher than all existing skyscrapers by 200 to 300 feet, and . . . about 40 feet higher than the Washington Monument."[*] Ernest Flagg's design was a confused, if romantic, variation on French Beaux-Arts precedents; with a slender tower shooting like an eager weed out a mansard-roofed base, it seemed like an attempt to clothe the dramatically new in architectural garb dramatically old. But as awkward as its form may have been, with the Singer Building all ideas of height were shattered: now a commercial building, an office tower, was not merely higher than Trinity Church's steeple (as the Pulitzer Building had been by a few feet), but so much higher that it rendered Trinity small. The Singer Building, like Trinity's steeple, was visible from all over town and it had an easily identifiable shape, making its great height all the more conspicuous. Only the tower's extreme narrowness—it was a mere 65 feet square until it bulged with ornament and its own mansard at the top—prevented it from having a more powerful impact on the cityscape.

The Singer Building was completed in 1908; it followed the 362-foot high Times Tower at Times Square of 1904, by Cyrus L. W. Eidlitz, and the 285-foot high Flatiron building at Madison Square of 1903, by Daniel H. Burnham and Company, both slender towers located on trian-

The St. Paul Building, New York. George B. Post, 1899.

* Quotations and factual information are referenced in the Notes section beginning on p. 167.

The Singer Building, New York.
Ernest Flagg, 1908.

The Singer tower's ornate mansard top.

gular islands in the midst of busy intersections and thus, like the Singer, not as overwhelming as their sheer height might suggest. But a new world was in the making, and far more significant to the direction in which skyscraper design was moving, though far less celebrated, were a number of the Singer Building's close neighbors—two 21-story Gothic near-twins, the Trinity Building at 111 Broadway and the United States Realty Building at 115 Broadway, both completed in 1906 to the designs of Francis H. Kimball, and 165 Broadway, a 34-story mass just north of Singer on Broadway, also designed by Kimball and also Gothic in detail. Number 165 Broadway was under construction at the same time as Singer, and the *New York Times* announced its beginning in the same front-page story with which it had heralded the taller Singer. "Some expectation had been entertained that this structure might gratify the public demand for some high point in the downtown landscape, but it will be a comparative dwarf alongside the Singer Tower," the *Times* said.

That a 34-story building could be considered a relatively minor event, worth noting only to record the subservient role it would play in the skyline to its neighbor, indicates how rapidly change was coming to lower Manhattan. Not only had height pushed up tremendously—the Flatiron and Times towers were proof of that—the relationship sky-

A 1908 postcard.

The Times Tower, New York. Cyrus L. W. Eidlitz, 1904.

7

"It was a time of intense, almost delirious growth." The Flatiron Building under construction.

scrapers were having to one another and to the city at large was altering dramatically. The skyscraper was coming less and less to mean sheer height, a thin tower rising alone amid smaller buildings; more and more it was coming to mean an enormous bulk, a huge mass set beside other huge masses. By the end of the first decade of the century the blocks of Manhattan's business district were being covered by identical structures; although unlike the identical structures that had blanketed these blocks in previous generations, the new buildings rose not six and seven stories, but 15 or 20 or 30 floors into the sky.

And they were different from buildings that had come before in much more than size. The new skyscrapers had more than just offices, floor after floor of desks and stenographers' tables; as the buildings grew they began to acquire stores and restaurants and bars, and their lobbies became so large that they were gathering places in themselves. "The massive arcades constitute a veritable city, with their varied shops, stores, counters, and sales places, vending most everything desired from fruits, food and candy, to wearing apparel, hardware, and household items," proclaimed a promotional piece on the Hudson Terminal Buildings, the twin masses on Church Street completed in 1908 to the design of Clinton and Russell. "One of the largest office buildings in the world—covers almost two square blocks, with bridges over Dey Street connecting the two huge structures at the 3rd and 17th stories," the literature exclaimed. The new buildings were truly, as Rem Koolhaas has pointed out, "a reproduction of the world."

To some, all of this represented progress at its best. "So swiftly do the wheels of progress revolve in New York that one great achievement may not be finished before another and more wonderful improvement is on the way. It is so with the two tallest skyscrapers ever constructed, and which are in the course of construction here," gloated the *New York Times* on December 29, 1907, taking note of the nearly completed Singer Tower and the recent start of construction of the 700-foot Metropolitan Life Tower at Madison Square, designed by Napoleon LeBrun and Sons. The city was growing, it was prospering; it was becoming to capitalism what Rome was to the Church, and the more the city's role as a vital commercial center could be expressed through huge buildings, the stronger would be its position.

It was a time of intense, almost delirious growth: not only did height seem to be conquered, so did all of the inconveniences and congestion of the traditional city. Skyscrapers would provide grandeur and views and also clean streets and efficient communication, or so it seemed to their enthusiasts; builder Theodore Starrett proposed in 1906 a hulking, boxy 100-story building that would include industry at the bottom, business in the next section, residences above, and a hotel above that, with each section separated by public plazas including theaters, shopping districts, and, at the top, an amusement park, roof garden, and swimming pool. "Our civilization is progressing wonderfully. In New York . . . we must keep building and we must build upward. Step by step we have advanced from the wooden hut to the 30-story skyscraper. . . . Now we must develop something different, something larger." In one famous rendering, "King's Dream of New York," drawn by Harry M. Pettit for guidebook publisher Moses King, the Singer Building is dwarfed by dozens of other skyscrapers, and the view up Broadway is punctuated by aerial bridges and multilevel rail systems. Dirigibles crisscross in the air, one headed

Opposite: The Flatiron Building, New York. Daniel H. Burnham and Company, 1903.

A drawing of Starrett's proposed 100-story building as it appeared in the New York Herald, *May 13, 1906.*

for Europe, the next one tying lower Manhattan to Japan. The East River is lined with great skyscrapers, in Brooklyn as well as in Manhattan. The only touch that mars the pure futurism of it is that King, like Ernest Flagg, seemed sure that skyscrapers were not essentially different in their architecture from most nineteenth-century buildings, and thus the rendering is a maze of turrets and cupolas and mansards and domes, a far cry indeed from the stark modernism that was to come to lower Manhattan not so many years later. But the historicism of King's vision made its romantic pull all the more powerful—and for years this rendering, widely reproduced, symbolized to the popular eye the new skyscraper city that New York was becoming.

Laissez-faire capitalism as housed in laissez-faire architecture did not please everyone, however, and as the great new towers neared completion an increasing amount of dissent could be heard. The city was in the process of revising its building code in 1908, and a special committee was charged with reviewing the issue of tall buildings. Surprisingly, Ernest Flagg, the Singer Building's architect, emerged as a strong advocate of legal limits to skyscrapers. Flagg told a City Hall hearing that he believed tall buildings should be restricted to three-quarters of their sites, thus assuring open ground area and adequate light, or else limited to no more than 100 feet in height. Towers could rise to any height if they covered no more than one-quarter of the plot. Flagg's plan would have led to more Singer-like slender towers, goosenecks craning into the sky, or, as Flagg himself put it, a skyline that would be a "tiara of proud towers." It would have also regulated the city, in a sense, creating an even 100-foot-high cornice line.

Flagg called as well for a system in which neighboring property owners could buy and sell air rights, thus limiting the actual number of high buildings and assuring that a particular district did not become overcrowded. This notion showed considerable prescience, for it resembles a number of schemes that were proposed in the 1960's in American cities; in 1908, Flagg's scheme got a polite hearing—a result of the architect's eminence as much as anything else, one suspects—but it did not get him much more.

Montgomery Schuyler, the distinguished architecture critic and correspondent of the *Architectural Record,* saw Flagg's proposal and a somewhat similar scheme advanced by David Knickerbocker Boyd, president of the Philadelphia chapter of the American Institute of Architects, as an encouraging sign that the architectural profession, which "may seem to have almost the most direct interest in the failure to restrict the height of buildings," was in fact offering to regulate itself. The real villain, Schuyler believed, was the real estate developer, who he feared would have no interest in esthetic guidelines or in size restrictions. "But to make your tall building a sightly or attractive object, this superficial treatment [the guidelines suggested by Flagg] is not sufficient. The aspiring dollar-hunter would continue to protrude stark parallelepipeds into the empyrean, just as he does now," Schuyler wrote in the *Record.* "And although it would be a very good and civic thing if the owners of the parallelopipeds were required to give them form and comeliness, and although such a requirement might be enforced by the prefecture of the Seine, it were a fond imagination that the individualistic New Yorker, whose rampant individualism is, in fact, in this matter, the source of all our woes, would submit to such a limitation of his right to do what he will with his own. The parallelepiped is the form which gives him the most space for rental and which can be most cheaply built. To prevent him from building it would seem to him a great outrage."

Stronger still were the views of the Committee of Congestion of Population in New York, a private organization seeking to put pressure on the Building Code Revision Commission to limit skyscrapers. The committee expressed shock in 1908 at plans filed by the Equitable Life Assurance Society for a 62-story, 909-foot skyscraper between Broadway and Nassau Street (a building that ended up being built in different, but ultimately more startling, form), arguing that the streets could not hold the traffic the building would generate. One anonymous member was quoted in the *New York Times* as saying, "To accommodate such a crowd the people would have to walk in three layers, one above the other, while the roadway would not hold the delivery wagons, automobiles, and carriages of people going to the structure." The committee proposed in August of 1908 that the city consider an absolute height restric-

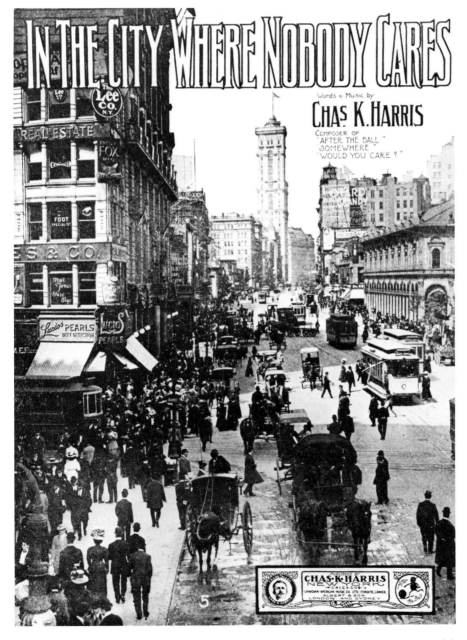

A piece of 1908 sheet music using a photograph of Broadway looking towards the Times Tower.

tion, a limit of tall buildings to certain districts, or a special tax on sky-scrapers.

And David Knickerbocker Boyd ardently promoted his plan not only through Schuyler's columns, but through his own writings. In *American Architecture and Building News,* Boyd was blunt. "Aside from all aesthetic considerations the continued erection of the so-called 'skyscraper,' the excessively tall building, constitutes a menace to public health and safety and an offence which must be stopped. Any further talk, there-fore, of the one thousand foot building and the two thousand foot limit of possible height, or of projects for 60-story buildings as recently ad-vanced, can only hasten the doom of these architectural protuberances. . . . In the present movement to correct the evil much has been said about shutting out the light of the heavens and circumscribing the air of

"What We Might Come To," an unknown artist's vision of the skyscraper's future.

the streets—to both of which possessions people are entitled, and which, in the pursuit of health, happiness, and prosperity, they should demand. This 'canyonizing' of the streets is rapidly being accomplished and its baleful results are beginning to forcibly assert themselves."

The fear that the skyscraper would put an end to the traditional street by closing it in had been expressed before. Indeed, the eminent architect George B. Post complained as far back as 1894 that streets, if lined with tall buildings, would seem like canyons, dark, gloomy, and damp. The renderings made for Moses King's guides underscored the point: they showed dark and menacing streets, a separate world altogether from the exuberant bridges leaping across rooftops. But his pessimism about the skyscraper-lined street was immediately contradicted by Daniel Burnham, Chicago's great entrepreneur-architect, who said he saw dark and gloomy streets as no problem, since modern technology could provide artificial light and ventilation.

From King's Views of New York.

But Schuyler's cynicism, not Burnham's almost innocent confidence, seems to have been the more accurate response: as the controversy mounted, so did the buildings, not merely in New York but in Chicago, in Philadelphia, and in smaller cities as well. Chicago enacted a 10-story height limit for a few years, then removed it; in 1906 the *Springfield* (Massachusetts) *Republican* called for a 100-foot height limitation for Springfield's buildings, arguing that "New York and Chicago would be far handsomer and healthier cities without 'the skyscrapers.'" The *New York Times* reported the *Republican*'s words and, while conceding that "the skyscraper is still 'ferae naturae' and it is highly desirable to bring it under the reign of law," it dismissed the notion of a 100-foot limit in New York as "oppressive and absurd." The *Times* realized that the huge buildings were an apt reflection of burgeoning capitalism; to restrict the structures, it suggested, would be to restrict the businesses that were housed in them and that were increasingly coming to regard them as symbolic of their own economic potency.

The rugged individualism of New York was, indeed, running rampant, making the problem—if it was to be seen as a problem—far more intense than even in Chicago. But it was, ironically, to be a Chicago architect who dealt the final blow to the laissez-faire era of skyscraper construction in New York and, by implication, in other cities as well. Ernest Graham, a partner of Daniel Burnham and the successor architect to Burnham's immense firm, proposed for the Equitable Life Assurance Society at 120 Broadway in the heart of the lower Manhattan financial district a building that would cover a full block and rise without setbacks to a height of 39 stories. It was massive, far vaster—if not higher—than anything New York or any other city had yet seen. With 1.2 million square feet of rentable space, it would be by far the largest office building in the world, and the huge structure, its great mass running east to west, would cast shadows for blocks around. The Equitable Building was finished in 1915, and it was indeed awesome, with a through-block vaulted lobby that was, and is, a veritable street; the vast number of people it housed assured that it would be alive with energy and movement. But the expanse above resembles nothing more than a great file cabinet, partitioned off with identical windows in an overwhelming but utterly banal façade. The building was erected on the site of an earlier Equitable Building destroyed by fire, and was not actually owned by the Equitable Life Assurance Society. It belonged rather to T. Coleman du Pont, a real

13

The Equitable Building, New York.
Ernest Graham, 1915.

14

estate investor and a member of the Delaware du Pont family, who had been encouraged by Louis Horowitz, the president of Thompson-Starrett, the builders, to put $10 million into the venture. Du Pont liked to refer to the vast structure as the "du Pont cottage."

The owners of neighboring structures mounted a feeble protest before construction, aware that the Equitable would rob their tenants of substantial light. When they suggested that the site be turned into a park, Horowitz laughed them out of his office, suggesting that they purchase the land and build the park themselves. But it is no surprise that the Equitable Building was not popular either so far as the public was concerned or the city's real estate interests. Not only did it create a glut of office space on the market but, much more important to history, its bulk stimulated the City of New York to legislate some sort of restrictions on skyscraper form and location. The first zoning ordinance in the nation was passed in 1916, in part as a result of Equitable; among its restrictions were limits to bulk intended to make another Equitable Building—which contained a total floor area more than 30 times the size of its land area—an impossibility. Taller skyscrapers would follow, and ones that managed to intrude on esthetic grounds more violently than Equitable had, but Graham's great box remained the ultimate early-twentieth-century expression of the skyscraper as nothing more than a device to cram more floors into the sky. It was built not as a monument, but as economic adventurism.

Indeed, one is tempted to think that Henry James foresaw Equitable when he wrote in 1907 of the growing skyline of Manhattan: "One story is good until another is told, and skyscrapers are the last word of economic ingenuity only till another word be written. This shall be possibly a word of still uglier meaning, but the vocabulary of thrift at any price shows boundless resources, and the consciousness of that truth, the consciousness of the finite, the menaced, the essentially *invented* state, twinkles ever, to my perception, in the thousand glassy eyes of these giants of the mere market."

Lower New York skyline from the East River, 1908. The Brooklyn Bridge is on the far right; the Singer tower rises above the other buildings on the left.

Chapter Two
Chicago Beginnings

If it took the vast, bulky skyscrapers of the decade that culminated in the Equitable Building to prompt, at last, some legal restrictions on skyscrapers, there was nonetheless no little worry in the years before about the form these buildings were taking. The 1894 Architectural League symposium indicated the depth of concern in the profession; even in the 1880's it was beginning to be understood that tall buildings were fundamentally different from what had been built before, that skyscrapers demanded not merely a different set of attitudes toward the making of cities but a different esthetic as individual buildings as well. Thomas Hastings, the eminent Beaux-Arts architect who, with his partner John M. Carrère, was to design the New York Public Library, called at the symposium for "perfect freedom in composition," and recognized that the skyscraper represented a building problem that could not be solved by delving into historical precedent. Legal restrictions, Hastings said, could solve only the urbanistic part of the problem, by creating a uniform ensemble. (Curiously, he refers to the ideal streetscape as possessing "a charming unity and monotony"; it is a reminder of how much values have changed that the word *monotony* has come to mean such a different thing in urban design now.) Hastings offered few real guidelines, however—his main point was to argue against dogma, and he had little to say about the form of individual buildings save to argue for freedom of expression.

The great theorists of the skyscraper, and the architects who were to create the real beginnings for an art of skyscraper design long before the great debate over the ethics of the skyscraper reached its climax, were not in New York but in Chicago. They were Louis Sullivan and John Wellborn Root. Both men believed in the Zeitgeist; they were convinced that a new technology of the skyscraper would create a new architecture. Sullivan, in particular, argued his case with elegant, if extravagant, prose. In a now-classic essay entitled "The Tall Office Building Artistically Considered," he argued against the use of historical elements in the skyscraper and called for the building to reflect what he believed were American impulses. It was not different in its way from what Le Corbusier was to call for a quarter century later in *Vers une Architecture*; Sullivan claimed that new kinds of buildings required new kinds of ar-

Louis Sullivan.

Opposite: Façade of the Chicago Stock Exchange. Adler and Sullivan, 1894.

The Wainwright Building, St. Louis. Adler and Sullivan, 1891.

chitectural expression, and that only by developing such new forms could architecture be "a living art." Then all of Sullivan's romanticism broke through as he proclaimed that the skyscraper "must be tall, every inch of it tall. The force and power of altitude must be in it, the glory and pride of exaltation must be in it. It must be every inch a proud and soaring thing, rising in sheer exaltation that from bottom to top it is a unit without a single dissenting line."

Sullivan's passion led him to the design of several of the greatest of early skyscrapers. His Wainwright Building of 1891 in St. Louis, done in partnership with Dankmar Adler, is 10 stories of brick and terra cotta, minuscule by the standards of the massive buildings of a decade or two later. But Sullivan managed to express height in a way that no one else could at the time: the Wainwright is not merely tall; it is *about* being tall—it is tall architecturally even more than it is physically. The building has a solid 2-story base, above which rise 7 stories of vertical piers in

18

brick with a line of windows in between. The spandrels—the panels below each window—are decorated with terra cotta ornament, and at the top the entire composition melds into a tight, crisp, and yet ornate terra cotta cornice.

What Sullivan managed to do here was create a façade that could not have existed on a short building. It is not merely a low building made bigger; it is a tall building in its very essence. The vertical emphasis is part of the reason for the Wainwright's success, but only the most obvious; what Sullivan was doing was not merely being vertical, but merging verticality, taming it almost, into a coherent overall composition. Thus the slightly recessed spandrels, foreshadowing a method of façade design that was to remain viable as many years afterward as Rockefeller Center, and thus the cornice, which joins with the base in creating a horizontal emphasis that offers just the right degree of counterpoint to the verticality. Sullivan's ornament, too, has a balancing role: its delicacy and fineness, as well as its basis in natural forms, are played off precisely against the sleekness of the major façade elements. The result is a nearly perfect composition, in which no element could be removed without seriously damaging the whole.

Wainwright is fundamentally a set of façades, which fit together into a tight cube; it is not impressive as a new kind of shape, and it did not represent any real technological innovation or spatial creativity. The façade's tripartite organization suggests, of course, a classical column, with its base, shaft, and capital, and that analogy was to be invoked frequently as an esthetic of skyscrapers developed. But it does Sullivan a disservice to suggest that this connection was foremost in his mind; it would not explain his subtle interweaving of horizontals and verticals, for example, or his ability to relate the structure as well as he has to the concerns of the street. For Sullivan's inspirations lay elsewhere, in impulses more truly romantic than classical. He had been deeply moved by Henry Hobson Richardson's Marshall Field Warehouse of 1887, in Chi-

Marshall Field Warehouse, Chicago.
Henry Hobson Richardson, 1887.

cago, a powerful mass, Romanesque in its form but tight and ordered in the same sense that a Renaissance palace was; Sullivan said of Marshall Field, which had vertical rows of windows finishing in arches, that it was like "a man that walks on two legs . . . a virile force . . . stone and mortar, here, spring into life," and this anthropomorphic analogy was his highest praise.

Wainwright was the culmination of several early developments of skyscraper design, by Sullivan and others. In the 1880's a number of masonry buildings were built that, esthetically at least, were similar to Richardson's Marshall Field building. Sullivan's own Wacker Warehouse in Chicago, completed in 1889, used Richardson's themes more directly than Wainwright did, but it had great arched entrances at street level and a smooth façade rather than Richardson's deep rustication; these two variations joined to make the building more primal, more primitive in feeling than Richardson's, and at the same time sleeker. More directly Richardsonian was Adler and Sullivan's Auditorium Building in Chicago, also of 1889, where the connection to Marshall Field is unmistakable—a rough-hewn façade, with a solid box, and pairs of windows in vertical rows culminating in arches to create a monumental effect at the middle levels, then narrower arches above. The Auditorium Theater has a spectacular, glittering interior that is one of Sullivan's ornamental triumphs: it is based on a series of arches that prefigure the great arches of Radio City Music Hall. But the Auditorium was also a precursor of the mixed-use buildings that would become popular in the twentieth

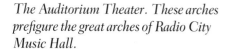

The Auditorium Theater. These arches prefigure the great arches of Radio City Music Hall.

The Auditorium Building, Chicago.
Adler and Sullivan, 1889.

century: it contained a hotel, an office tower, and performing arts facilities. Unlike Equitable, the Auditorium emerged out of a feeling that large buildings should enrich the city.

Not dissimilar esthetically, though narrower in function, was the Rookery, also in Chicago, by Burnham and Root, completed in 1886. Here, in an office block on Chicago's LaSalle Street, John Wellborn Root took the Richardsonian style and made it, if such is possible, somewhat decorative; there are turrets and capitals, an overlay of delicacy altogether unexpected in this heavy, masculine style. This was with no compromise to quality, for if the Rookery lacks the sense of cohesion of Richardson's or Sullivan's work, it has an extraordinary grace to it—this building seems, for all its weight, to dance. It was Root's genius here to be able to compose a façade that appeared light without being frivolous, welcoming without being obsequious. The Rookery is remarkable for its interior as well—it originally contained a glass-covered dome in its lobby, which remains a splendid central court, although since 1905 the glass has been painted over. Frank Lloyd Wright supervised the redesign of the lobby, and there are a number of Wrightian details, which merge neatly with Root's decorative ironwork.

John Wellborn Root, who was Daniel Burnham's partner and chief designer until his untimely death, at 40, in 1891, was Sullivan's colleague in the early development of the skyscraper. Their ideas were parallel, though their styles—personal and architectural—were not altogether identical. Both men insisted on the notion that the skyscraper should in some way express the nature of its construction, the idea of height, and the spirit of a new industrial society, but Root tended to be calmer and more empirical in his approach, whereas Sullivan saw the new style as something that would emerge, full-blown, from his drafting table. "Architectural styles . . . were never discovered by human prospectors," Root wrote in 1890. "Styles are found truly at the appointed time, but solely by those who, with intelligence and soberness, are working out their ends with the best means at hand, and with scarce a thought of the coming new or national style."

Louis Sullivan drawing of a detail used
in the Auditorium.

21

The Rookery, Chicago. Burnham and Root, 1886.

Root had begun his quest to give form to the tall building with a structure completed in 1882 in Chicago, the Montauk Building. This was a pioneering skyscraper—elevators permitted it to rise to 10 stories—yet it makes clear how little, thus far, architects had been able to give new form to what they were doing, for the Montauk is essentially 10 horizontal floors piled on top of each other. A 2-story arched entrance was an early, if desperate, attempt to give the building some sense of scale, but this is fundamentally a little building made big. So is William LeBaron Jenney's vaguely Romanesque 10-story Home Insurance Building of 1885, which also emphasizes horizontality and has no façade elements that could not have been present in a smaller building. The significance of the Home Insurance is in terms not of esthetics, but of technology, for this is the first tall building to be supported on a skeleton frame, in this case a mix of iron and steel.

The frame, to some historians, marks the beginning of the skyscraper. Without the steel frame, obviously, the truly high building

The Rookery lobby in the late 1880's.

could not exist, for the thickness of self-supporting masonry walls would be prohibitive when buildings reached major heights. But the frame alone is not an altogether comfortable beginning point for the skyscraper for a number of reasons. First, the steel frame did not appear all of a piece in Chicago's Home Insurance Building; it developed slowly, derived in part from the prefabricated cast-iron fronts that were popular in the middle decades of the nineteenth century, façades that were true frames, almost like twentieth century curtain walls, and that were given up later in the century only because they were not fireproof. Moreover, the other elements defining a skyscraper—the use of the elevator and the expression of height—occur frequently in buildings that precede the steel skeleton and even in many that follow its introduction but do not employ it.

There is no neat answer, then, to the question of what building was the first skyscraper. The Home Insurance Building introduced the steel skeleton, and contained elevators, but did not represent any design advances; much earlier had come the Equitable Building in New York (altogether different, except in name, from the giant Equitable of 1915), which was completed way back in 1870 by Gilman and Kendall, with George B. Post as engineer. This structure rose only to 6 stories, but they were high ones indeed, for the building's roof was 130 feet above the street; and more important still, the Equitable was the first office building to contain an elevator. Its style was ornate Second Empire, complete with mansard roof, so in terms of architectural expression of height, the Equitable was more conservative even than Montauk or Home Insurance—but it was tall, and did contain an elevator, thus bringing about the almost revolutionary occurrence of top floors that were as desirable as lower ones. After Equitable it began to be fashionable to be on a high floor, and this was a dramatic shift.

If Home Insurance is significant for its steel frame, and Equitable for its elevator, one further "partial skyscraper" building must be considered before we return to the generation of buildings that, like Wainwright, contain all three essential elements. This is the Monadnock of

The Home Insurance Building, Chicago. William LeBaron Jenney, 1885.

23

The bay windows of the Monadnock emphasize verticality.

1891, in Chicago, by Burnham and Root; along with the Rookery it was Root's masterpiece, and it was here that his ideas came together with clarity and strength. The Monadnock, oddly, is not a steel-frame building; it is the last of the great solid-masonry–walled structures, yet it is a skyscraper as surely as any of Sullivan's works. For here the powerful brick walls rise to 16 stories, smooth and clean in a way that must have appeared startling to nineteenth-century eyes. The walls are thick and heavy at the bottom and then, as if to express the diminishing weight they bear as they rise, they taper to thinness. There is no ornament whatsoever—just the gentle curve of the walls, and the shallow billows of rows of bay windows, which serve to emphasize verticality, not so directly as Sullivan's projecting piers but effectively nonetheless. The overall shape of the building, thanks to the 202-by-68-foot site, is a thin slab, making the Monadnock seem all the more like a much later building. But most important are the walls, monumentally powerful, hand-edged in a way that calls to mind not only much of the industrial brickwork of the later decades of the nineteenth century, but even the abstract minimalism of the twentieth.

Chicago's primacy as the city of the skyscrapers in the two closing decades of the century cannot be denied. Not only were the two great theorists of the skyscraper, Sullivan and Root, at work in that city, but so were a number of other architects of distinction—their partners Adler and Burnham; Frank Lloyd Wright, who came to devote great attention in later years to the skyscraper; and William Holabird and Martin Roche, who were to join in partnership and become, after John Root's death, as significant a presence in the downtown architectural scene of Chicago as Burnham and Root had been.

The mood and spirit of Chicago and New York were altogether different. Indeed, in these decades traits were developing in both cities that would shape their architectural identities well into the twentieth century. Chicago was a city intent on rebuilding itself rapidly after the disastrous fire of 1871; there was little in the way of tradition, architectural or cultural, to give direction to this process. It was a city of commerce, but its commerce was of the American heartland, not international trade; the city was always more hospitable to the seller of goods or the maker of machinery than to the intellectual or the traveler. Chicago sought culture, but was rapidly building confidence in its own inherent quality as a maker of culture—it did not seek to confirm its cultural status largely through what it might import from elsewhere.

Above all, in these decades Chicago was a young city—its own historical age was young, and the median age in 1880 of the architects who were most active in designing its new skyscrapers was only 30. The architects were for the most part free of the academic training that had formed the viewpoints of their Eastern colleagues. Sullivan had studied at the Ecole des Beaux Arts, but Root and Adler were primarily engineers, committed to a certain pragmatism that was not at all inconsistent with their city's character.

It was, in short, an extraordinary blend of energy and confidence, of intelligence and freshness of outlook, that marked Chicago in the 1880's. It was the frontier, yet it was also an established city, and a sense of both permeated it. There was in addition a bit of luck—not only in these architects' coming together here, but in Richardson's mature and influential work having occurred there, and in the fact that Peter and

Opposite: The Monadnock Building, Chicago. Burnham and Root, 1891.

129,677

Equitable Life Assurance Company Building, New York. Gilman, Kendall, and Post, 1870.

Shepard Brooks, Boston real estate investors, were committed to the new commercial style and built actively in Chicago. The Brookses saw in the austerity of the Chicago style a certain degree of economy as well as esthetic value, but they were serious and deeply committed to architectural quality. It was they who built the Montauk, the Rookery, and the Monadnock, among other works. They were Burnham and Root's great early patrons.

In Chicago, moreover, the more ordered layout of streets led to a more ordered city. New York's skyscrapers were set amid the narrow, crooked lanes of lower Manhattan, whereas Chicago's were on even, neat blocks in the Loop, creating a coherent overall pattern. In New York the skyscrapers seemed to compete; in Chicago, to cooperate.

The distinction was not lost on writers of the period, one of whom, novelist William Archer, wrote, "As the elephant . . . to the giraffe, so is the colossal business block of Chicago to the skyscraper of New York. There is a proportion and dignity in the mammoth of Chicago which is lacking in most of those which form the jagged skyline of Manhattan Island. Before the lanky giants of the Eastern metropolis, one has generally to hold one's esthetic judgement in abeyance. . . . They are simply astounding manifestations of human energy and heaven-storming audacity."

New York, for all its striving after height, seemed to care little for expression of technological innovation: it was there, after all, at the early Equitable Building, that the first office-building elevator was inserted into an ornate Second Empire structure. If Chicago looked to itself for inspiration, New York looked to Europe, reproducing Renaissance palazzi and Gothic towers and Georgian manor houses, taking all that it could from history. The notion of structural "honesty," of the frank expression of physical structure that was so important to Chicagoans, had little equivalent in New York, where pure visual pleasure was more the goal. There were two kinds of New York skyscrapers—those on which great attention had been lavished, which were pieces of theater as much as real estate, and those which were little more than devices for making money, systems for building rentable floors in the air.

The paradox of New York's devotion to flamboyant effect on the one hand and crass money-making on the other need not be dealt with here; suffice it to say that neither aspect of this city's double-edged character had a precise equivalent in Chicago. In neither case was there the sense of control that was ever present in Chicago—something always seemed to burst out in New York, whether in terms of height or ornament or sheer, voluminous mass.

Thus, following Equitable, we have such early New York skyscrapers as George B. Post's Western Union Building and Richard Morris Hunt's Tribune Building, both completed in 1875 and both remarkably similar. Western Union was 10 stories high and the Tribune, 9; each had a mansard roof, an elaborate and highly picturesque central tower, and lavish ornament. The buildings were monuments of high Victoriana in one sense, but in another they were brazen new skyscrapers, pushing 230 and 260 feet into the air and, in the case of Western Union at least, indicating a considerable attempt to express verticality through tall piers flanking the windows. There were no steel frames here, of course, and the style was unabashedly historicist—but these buildings were powerful statements of height seven years before Root's Montauk and more

than a decade before Richardson's Marshall Field.

New York continued to build actively through the 1880's, but there was little of real note; the steel frame came late to the city, first used in 1889 by Bradford Gilbert in the Tower Building on lower Broadway. The name was eager but misguided, for the building was in fact a slab, with its narrow end set on Broadway and appearing rather like a tower; it was topped with some crude ornament that made vague reference to medieval castles. It is a structure of purely historical interest, and it is worth noting here that, for all of New York's quick start at skyscraper building in the 1870's, it took four years for the crucial technological element of very tall buildings—the steel frame—to make its way from Chicago back east.

Chicago's commercial style, established firmly in the 1880's, continued to grow and mature through the following decade. In 1892 came Burnham and Root's Masonic and Women's temples, the former 22 stories high and briefly the world's tallest building. Both were openly Romanesque, representing a retreat, in a sense, from the sleekness of the Monadnock. Both buildings also contained elaborate, chateau-like tops, suggesting that Root was deeply conscious of the issue of a climax to his vertical composition—though, ironically, his solution resembled the work of the New York historicists more than that of his Chicago colleagues.

The culminating structures of Chicago's early period of skyscraper design were built during the middle of the decade. There was Adler and Sullivan's Stock Exchange of 1894, its great arched entrance now pre-

New York's Newspaper Row. City Hall (Joseph Mangin and John McComb, Jr., 1811) is on the left; the World Building (George B. Post, 1890) and the Tribune Building (Richard Morris Hunt, 1875) are in the middle; and the Times Building is on the right.

27

served, pathetically, as an empty work of sculpture on the grounds of the Art Institute of Chicago, and its trading floor restored within. In the same year the Stock Exchange was completed the Reliance Building, designed by Charles B. Atwood of Burnham and Company, opened its doors; here, for the first time since the cast-iron fronts of decades before, glass becomes everything. Set within the Reliance's terra cotta frame are huge sheets of glass, and the façade has an extraordinary lightness, even a transparency, to it. It prefigures the glass skyscrapers of the mid-twentieth century, breaking as dramatically with precedent as did Skidmore, Owings, and Merrill's Lever House or Pepsi-Cola headquarters, its true comrades.

If the Reliance pointed the way toward the future, brilliantly and briefly (it was not to be imitated or repeated), another great building of 1894, the Marquette, summarized the past. This was among Holabird and Roche's first major works; it might be called the Platonic Chicago Building, for it seems to be the ideal expression of the mature Chicago commercial style. It is a handsome, serenely proportioned structure,

The Chicago Stock Exchange. Adler and Sullivan, 1894.

The Reliance Building, Chicago.
Burnham and Company, 1894.

which sits on the street with a combination of strength and grace that can only call to mind the Rookery. There is a strong base, a sleek midsection with slightly recessed spandrels, and an elaborate and vaguely classicized cornice. The E-shaped floor plan is purely functional, spreading light and air widely through the interior. Most important, here the expression of the steel frame on the outside comes truly into its own—the thick vertical columns on the exterior are cladding over supporting columns inside, and where there are no columns within, the windows are divided only by thin metal mullions. The result was what became known as the "Chicago window"—a wide expanse of glass, with large fixed panes in the center and two operable windows at the ends.

The development of the Chicago skyscraper form did continue through the decade. Sullivan, whose greatest achievements in skyscraper design seemed, ironically, to take place outside of Chicago, created what could reasonably be called his masterpiece in 1895, with the Guaranty (now Prudential) Building in Buffalo. The forms are similar to those that burst through with such freshness in the Wainwright; here, however, the building has been stretched to 13 stories so it appears, at last, a true tower and not a cube. The treatment of the top is more graceful, too, with Sullivan's lush ornament seeming to grow out of the arches that top each vertical row of windows and then swirl about the round

The base of the Guaranty Building with its specially designed storefront windows, bent back at the top, seeming "to lift the entire structure into the air."

30

The Guaranty Building, Buffalo. Adler and Sullivan, 1895.

windows of the uppermost story before disappearing into a covelike cornice. More remarkable still is Sullivan's base, which here, thanks to an innovative design for the shopfronts involving windows bent back at the top, seems to lift the entire structure into the air. The Guaranty thus seems at once to represent the triumph of soaring, cohesive Chicago skyscraper design and to prefigure the skyscrapers of the International Style, which are raised off the ground on pilotis.

The rest of the decade belonged to Sullivan. He was working alone by then, his partnership with Adler having dissolved; it was the beginning of a long slide downward for the prophet of the skyscraper, who died in poverty in 1924, and in his last years had no large-scale commissions at all, designing only a series of tiny, though deeply moving, small-town

31

32

Midwestern banks. However, there were still major works through the turn of the century, including Sullivan's only structure in New York City, the Bayard Building of 1898, on Bleecker Street.

Bayard is all in the façade; the sides and rear are conventional. But it is a lilting, magical front, more delicate than either Wainwright or Guaranty. Sullivan distinguished here between bearing and nonbearing structural columns, and thus the façade alternates between thick and thin vertical lines, telling us at a glance how the building is made. It is more delicate, if less powerful, than the two earlier skyscrapers; the cornice contains six angels, ornament far more literal than Sullivan's usual, and one wonders if Sullivan's goal was in part a mockery of New York City's tendency toward picturesque decoration. It would be neat and dramatic personal architectural history if it were so—but in fact the ornament derives from an earlier Adler and Sullivan scheme, the unbuilt project for the Trust and Savings Building in St. Louis of 1893. This building was to have contained shopfronts similar to those at the Guaranty, recessed though not continuous vertical window mullions, and a cornice remarkably like that of the Bayard Building. Had it been built, it might well be considered among the architect's masterpieces.

Back in Chicago, Sullivan designed a façade for the Gage Building, the northernmost of a trio of small buildings on South Michigan Avenue by Holabird and Roche. The Holabird and Roche structures, completed

Three buildings by Holabird and Roche on South Michigan Avenue, Chicago. The façade of the Gage Building, on the right, is by Louis Sullivan, 1899.

Opposite: The Bayard Building, New York. Louis Sullivan, 1898.

33

in 1899, were a straightforward and handsome example of the Chicago style, crisp slices of the Marquette Building set beside Grant Park. Sullivan's façade, also of 1899, is flamboyant, with the structural columns clearly expressed, as at Bayard, but here topped by massive explosions of ornament. These ornamental bursts, which Vincent Scully has likened to brooches, appear, in his view, to be holding up the columns, "the window frames clattering down between them like Venetian blinds." But the ornamental tops also seem to be finishing off the columns, as if this rich design were shooting out of their shafts like water from a geyser.

Sullivan was to create one more major work in Chicago, the Carson Pirie Scott Department Store, completed in stages from 1901 to 1904. Here the movement is all horizontal, with a crispness that no other Sullivan building contains; it defines the street with a kind of streamlined majesty that was in its way as far ahead of its time as the Wainwright had been. The store is entered through a round corner tower, which is the one vertical element in the composition; the door is surrounded with a lavish outpouring of Sullivan's curvilinear ornament, so that one feels as if one is plunging into a den of rich, sensuous webbing. There is a small entry lobby, which has recently been skillfully restored, a demonstration of the continued respect the store's owners feel for the building—a masterpiece beloved by all Chicago still.

Carson Pirie Scott Department Store, Chicago. Louis Sullivan, 1901–04.

Opposite: The Carson Pirie Scott main entrance.

34

WOOLWORTH BUILDING C-9352
B'way & Park Place
Copyright 1913 By
IRVING UNDERHILL. N.Y.

CHAPTER THREE

NEW YORK AS THEATER

The Carson Pirie Scott store closed out a chapter in the history of architecture as firmly as it closed out one in the life of Louis Sullivan, for it was the last major achievement by the architect who had given Chicago a recognizable skyscraper style. Leadership after the turn of the century passed to New York, and that city's leanings toward theatrics began to play a greater and greater role in the overall evolution of the skyscraper. The first Equitable, the Western Union, and the Tribune buildings were the starting points, flamboyant structures that owed much more to the stage-set impulse than to the drive toward a rigorous theory of the skyscraper that had motivated the Chicagoans. Yet the New York buildings were as rich, if not as intellectually disciplined, as their Chicago counterparts; not only were they visually more ornate, but they were able, in a way that the Chicago buildings could do only occasionally, to communicate on several levels simultaneously. They symbolized at once the power of technology and the power of history—or, to put it another way, they expressed the belief of their corporate owners and tenants that an adaption of the new technology did not have to mean an abandonment of tradition. They were buildings for owners—and members of the public—who wanted all the glory of the past along with all of the promise of the future, for those who wished, in an architectural sense, to have their cake and eat it, too.

The New York skyscrapers were long ignored by architectural historians, who tended to see them as misguided attempts to graft historical forms onto modern frames. But it seems increasingly clear that this art of grafting, although shocking to orthodox modernists who see the skyscraper only as an expression of height and technology, could be remarkably skillful—an achievement that, at its best, deserves to rank nearly with that of Sullivan.

The curious mix of esthetic pretension and ruthless profiteering that characterized New York during the early years of the twentieth century led, as we have seen, to bitter arguments, not merely over the quality of skyscrapers but over the morality of their very existence. New York was a city of some anarchy so far as planning was concerned. But these years before World War I also brought, amid the great hulks that blotted out the sky, not a few distinguished buildings. Among them was surely a

Opposite: The Woolworth Building, New York. Cass Gilbert, 1913.

Edward Steichen's portrait of the Flatiron Building.

A popular postcard view of the downdrafts at the Flatiron.

skyscraper that must rank among the very greatest ever created—the Woolworth Building.

Ernest Flagg's Singer Building and Burnham's Flatiron building were the spiritual parents of all the ornate, eclectic skyscrapers that were to rise high in Manhattan in those years. The Flatiron, completed in 1903, represented a retreat from the innovative work that carried Burnham's name in the days of his partnership with Root; here an ornate French Renaissance blanket of ornament covers the façade like a great shimmering curtain. But if clarity of structural expression was not Burnham's first priority, the Flatiron's remarkable triangular shape made it a real esthetic triumph, as much a symbol of the New York skyline for its time as the Empire State Building was for a later one.

The shape, which probably emerged out of Burnham's prognostic desire to fill up the small triangular plot at the intersection of Broadway and 23rd Street, makes the Flatiron rise with a stunning lightness. The apex of the triangle is only six feet wide, and from certain vantage points the building appears more a thick wall than a volume, for the angles of the triangle erase any sense of depth. More important still, the building rises as a sheer tower, unencumbered by neighboring structures, large or small. It is, in a sense, what every Manhattan tower aspires to but few have ever been able to achieve.

The building rapidly became an icon of Manhattan, and a subject of seemingly endless interest for photographers and artists. Edward Steichen and Alfred Stieglitz, among others, saw the Flatiron as a mystical tower, rising softly out of the haze, almost a part of the natural landscape. But the building intrigued the public just as much—the high tower created downdrafts, and in the early years of the Flatiron's existence, when female fashion required full-length skirts, a popular male pastime was to linger at the base of the building and watch the wind flap petticoats into the air. Legend has it that the phrase "Twenty-three Skiddoo" derived from the shouts of policemen charged with clearing 23rd Street of Flatiron gawkers.

The Flatiron represented an early move north of the skyscraper district, and for some years it had no rivals in height among its immediate neighbors. There was, of course, the Times Tower of 1904 at Times Square, by Cyrus L. W. Eidlitz, taller still and possessed of a triangular site similar to that of the Flatiron. But the Times Tower, even before it was brutally renovated by Haines Lundberg Waehler in 1966, never possessed the grace of the Flatiron; it had a certain amiable quality to it, but never a soaring one.

Then in 1909 came the 700-foot Metropolitan Life Tower, in which New York's historicist tendencies achieved a new extreme. For here Napoleon LeBrun and Sons produced a virtual replica, on a vastly larger scale, of the Campanile in St. Mark's Square in Venice—though architect Pierre LeBrun tried to deny the direct connection, telling the *New York Times* rather disingenuously, "An architect cannot be said blindly to copy one building from another. He studies every type of building and learns all he can about them. The impressions he receives are bound to appear in his subsequent works, that's all. . . . [It is] no more than so-called 'unconscious absorption.'"

Whether this convinced the *Times* is not recorded, though the year before LeBrun's comment, the paper's correspondent, upon viewing plans for the unfinished tower, did explain in print that the Metropoli-

The Metropolitan Life Tower, New York. Napoleon LeBrun and Sons, 1909.

The Campanile in St. Mark's Square, Venice.

tan Tower and the Campanile "might be called twin sisters." But the writer went on to note, "There is a vital difference: Two Venetian campaniles might be placed one on top of the other, yet they would not be as high as the Metropolitan Life Tower."

The Metropolitan Life was not the first time that an architect had looked to the Campanile for a solution to the skyscraper problem. George B. Post, the skyscraper opponent, had proposed a similarly derivative tower, though with more connection to the tower of the Houses of Parliament in London, in 1899 for Metropolitan Life's rival, the Prudential Life Insurance Company. And before that, in 1890, Bruce Price had turned to the Campanile at St. Mark's for a 30-story tower, which, like the Prudential, was never realized.

The decision to replicate a well-known historical structure, and yet to do so at a scale that broke completely with precedent, was indicative of the extent to which skyscrapers were being called upon to play symbolic roles. To the Metropolitan Life Insurance Company, the tower confirmed its stability and suggested that the qualities of past cultures had somehow been passed along to it, that the twentieth-century corporation was not merely a guardian of culture, it was possessor of it, controller of it, as its ability to replicate the tower at a scale larger than the original proved.

The Metropolitan Life Tower, for all its historical cribbing, was a handsome and effective element on the city skyline. Like the Flatiron, this tower stood alone, rising narrow and free, its profile an easily identi-

Customs House Tower, Boston.
Peabody and Stearns, 1915.

Bankers Trust Company, New York.
Trowbridge and Livingston, 1912.

fiable symbol. The huge clock, its face three stories high, enhanced the tower's role as a benign element in the cityscape, which it continues to be—an unpleasant renovation completed in 1964 that involved the removal of a substantial amount of its façade ornament notwithstanding.

The Campanile had a brief fashion after the Metropolitan Life's completion. Its most notable, and bizarre, example was in Boston, where in 1915 the architectural firm of Peabody and Stearns thrust a narrow tower atop the old Customs House, eliminating the dome but retaining the original Doric portico as an entrance. It is a classical temple that has grown a modern offshoot, and despite Peabody and Stearns's zealous use of classical details, the clash of scale and building types is never resolved.

Not least of the lessons the awkward building taught was how good its predecessor, the Metropolitan Tower, was by comparison. Much better, if only by virtue of its proportions, was the thicker tower designed by Trowbridge and Livingston and completed in 1912 for the Bankers Trust Company of New York. A pyramidal top was the theme here, set over a colonnade of Ionic columns that topped a long shaft of unadorned windows. The relatively simple geometric crown has remained the corporate symbol of the bank, even though its headquarters has since moved elsewhere.

Far more significant in the development of the historicist skyscraper was a building commissioned by the City of New York to house its growing bureaucracy, which had long since outgrown the exquisite, tiny City Hall of 1811. The Municipal Building, completed in 1913, was designed by McKim, Mead, and White, which won the commission as a result of an architectural competition. The architect was William M. Kendall, a partner in the firm; Charles McKim himself had little to do with the project, a result of both his ill health (he died in 1909, just after the design was completed) and of his general lack of interest in skyscraper de-

The Municipal Building, New York. McKim, Mead, and White, 1913.

41

sign. The building is an attempt to mix the rather grandiose, Beaux-Arts–influenced classicism that had become the McKim firm's trademark with the skyscraper form. It is shaped like a flattened U, so that it appears from a distance to embrace the old City Hall to the southwest. It straddles Chambers Street with a great arch (crossing the street was a condition of the competition program, not an innovation of this design), giving the building not only a triumphal entrance but also a profound urbanistic presence. This is a skyscraper that the city passes *through*, not merely around. Making its relationship to the urban context more intimate still is the presence of a subway entrance in an open arcade of the ground floor; it is the predecessor of every lobby integrated with a mass transit facility that appeared in later generations.

The building was more advanced urbanistically than architecturally. But the grand scale and skillful, not to mention earnest, use of classical elements make up for the lack of real innovation. The form is the classic tripartite division—a 3-story base, here expressed with engaged Corinthian columns that break away to form an open colonnade across the U; a simple, almost bland shaft; and an ornate two-part capital, which consists of a row of columns along the upper floors of the main mass of the building, and then, set on the center, a 9-story sequence of colonnaded towers, surmounted by Adolph Weinman's statue "Civic Fame."

Classical tempietto mounting upon tempietto to a central climax give the top something of a wedding-cake finish, and the relationship of all this to the rest of the building is less than ideal (the top is an ornamental fillip more than it is a logical outgrowth of the form of the 27 stories of the main mass); but here, perhaps more than anywhere else, an architect attempted to erect a skyscraper that would be a classicizing civic monument like the courthouses and banks of the age. The Municipal Building brings the values of the City Beautiful movement—classical forms, noble civic spaces—to the skyscraper.

Far more resolved as a single work was the building that must be considered the masterpiece of this eclectic age in New York, the Woolworth Building. Cass Gilbert, a Beaux-Arts architect whose experience in designing tall structures had heretofore been relatively minor, took on the assignment of designing the world's tallest building as a symbol of one of the world's most successful retail corporations. The building was completed in 1913. It rose to 792 feet, and it was paid for by Woolworth with $13.5 million—in cash. There has never been a mortgage, and it has never passed out of the ownership of the F. W. Woolworth Company, which maintains its offices there still.

Woolworth's style was Gothic, a style that Gilbert had begun to explore with a previous attempt at skyscraper design, the West Street Building of 1907. West Street was a massive tower that managed, thanks to Gilbert's delicate detailing, to give an impression of considerable lightness. More important even than physical weight, however, was verticality—the Gothic style's insistent, almost urgent shouts upward seemed particularly appropriate for the skyscraper. And though Gilbert sought no expression of structure, as Sullivan had, he ended up with it anyway—the vertical piers of West Street, designed as imitations of Gothic structural elements, bear a striking resemblance to Sullivan's own verticals, and the building lifts upward with genuine, if fussy, grace.

West Street was an essay toward the full idea realized in Woolworth, where the excessive ornamental activity of the West Street façade is

Cass Gilbert, as he appears in one of the gargoyles in the lobby of the Woolworth Building.

Woolworth tower and Navy dirigible.

toned down, subdued into an even, serene vertical expression. It is not literally Gothic—there is obviously no medieval model for it—but it is zealously Gothic in its details, down to terra cotta gargoyles and buttresses. Most important, if it can be separated from the detail, is the massing. This element makes Woolworth one of the most remarkable skyscrapers ever built—a building so well composed that it is at once perceived as a sheer tower, like Metropolitan Life, and as an urban block set among other urban blocks, like Wainwright. The building's base is a 29-story, U-shaped mass, with the open side of the U facing west, away from the building's front on Broadway. Rising from the center of the front is a square tower, which sets back twice before the top, where it culminates in an ornate pinnacled crown.

Here, all of the awkwardness of Ernest Flagg's Singer, to take one example, is resolved. The slender tower seems not an overeager misfit, dropped onto a short building that would have preferred not to have had it, but a natural outgrowth of the base. It is not set back at all from the façade, and the vertical lines of the base shoot upward into the tower, melding the upper and lower masses together. The thin white lines of the terra cotta ornament stream skyward, looking as if they could go on forever.

43

The Woolworth's Gothic top.

The mix of delicacy and strength has an almost Mozartian quality to it, a sense of light, graceful detail applied to a firm and self-assured structure. Later critics, such as William Jordy, have correctly pointed out that the façade has none of the rigorous clarity of Sullivan's vertically expressive skyscrapers, but it seems to be no less an accomplishment for lack of this, and at its completion the building was received with considerable acclaim. There was a general sense among architects and critics of the period that at last an architect had done it—had found a way to express height, to create a work that was stylistically appropriate to the new forms. By 1913, in New York at least, the theoretical innovations of Chicago were of relatively little interest, and it was clear that if a skyscraper was to have any style to it, any form other than that of a massive block, it would have to have some sort of historical reference. Classicism, as at the Municipal Building, seemed awkward; French Beaux-Arts, as at Singer, no more natural—but the Gothic style seemed, after Woolworth, to be the New York architect's salvation. In this mode he might build tall, soaring buildings that felt like skyscrapers and nothing else—yet he could avoid the break with history that the Chicagoans, whose work he had often felt had been utilitarian at best, had been advocating. Even the great critic Montgomery Schuyler, who was more inclined to be respectful to the Chicago commercial style than many New Yorkers, wrote that in comparison with European Gothic churches, "this brand new American Gothic loses nothing." And Schuyler went on to celebrate the virtues of the Gothic over the other period styles: "One can hardly refrain from asking himself whether a comparable success with that of the latest and greatest of our skyscrapers can be attained within the repertory of our Parisianized architecture."

Cass Gilbert had no pretense of using Gothic detail for anything other than purely compositional purposes. As he said, "To me a skyscraper, by its height which makes its upper parts appear lost in the clouds, is a monument whose masses must become more and more inspired the higher it rises. The Gothic style gave us the possibility of expressing the greatest degree of aspiration . . . the ultimate note of the mass gradually gaining in spirituality the higher it mounts."

The building's popular fans, of which there were many, were more inclined to give deeper meaning to the Gothic style than was Gilbert. "It inspires feelings even too deep for tears," wrote the Reverend S. Parker Cadman, who proceeded to dub the structure "The Cathedral of Commerce"—a nickname that, not surprisingly, so satisfied the Woolworth Company that in 1917 it published a brochure about the building with that as its title.

Much of the brochure was devoted to facts and figures of the sort that were coming increasingly to captivate the popular imagination. The Woolworth housed 14,000 workers, and the area visible from its tiny fifty-eighth–floor crow's-nest observation platform (long since closed to the public) embraced a population of 9,500,000. The building's generating plant could supply electric lights for a city of 50,000; the boiler had a capacity of 2,500 horsepower, and the bunkers could store 2,000 tons of coal. The elevators were the fastest then known, and there were 29 of them, including two that operated express from the ground floor to the fifty-fourth floor, the largest rise of any elevator in the world. The brochure devoted four full pages to a discussion of the safety of the Woolworth's elevators, an indication that this was of even greater concern to

Opposite: Gothic detail was used inside too. The Woolworth elevators.

44

45

the public than the fact that the building contained 2,800 telephones, received 150,000 pieces of mail per day, and weighed 223,000 pounds.

But it is the Reverend Cadman who gives the final evidence of the public's acceptance of the Woolworth Building. Cadman wrote the foreword to "The Cathedral of Commerce," and he made no attempt to separate God from Mammon: "Just as religion monopolized art and architecture during the Medieval epoch, so commerce has engrossed the United States since 1865. . . . Out of the struggle of this process . . . have been developed gratifying benefits. . . . Here, on the Island of Manhattan, and at its southerly extremity, stands a succession of buildings without precedent or peer. . . . Of these buildings, the Woolworth is Queen, acknowledged as premier by all lovers of the city and the commonwealth, by critics from near and far, by those who aspire toward perfection, and by those who use visible things to obtain it."

The Woolworth lobby.

Opposite: The Woolworth Building in the foreground and the Municipal Building in the background bracket New York's Post Office Building and City Hall.

CHAPTER FOUR
THE TOWERS COME TOGETHER

By the First World War, the skyscraper had become an established fact of urban existence, not merely in New York and Chicago but in most cities throughout the United States. Most skyscrapers were designed by prosperous commercial architectural firms, organizations like Chicago's vast Burnham and Company, later Graham, Anderson, Probst, and White, or the office of Francis H. Kimball, the New York architect who designed the huge buildings at 111, 115, and 165 Broadway and seemed to specialize in the creation of vast blocks of space for real estate entrepreneurs.

But the problem of designing a tall building was increasingly coming to intrigue other architects as well—architects whose work was more oriented to the theoretical than to the commercial side of architecture and whose skyscraper designs were not the result of commissions from real estate developers for actual buildings. Frank Lloyd Wright, for example, whose practice consisted largely, though not exclusively, of houses, had been fascinated by the skyscraper since his days as an apprentice to Louis Sullivan; in 1895 he produced a scheme for a 10-story skyscraper that expressed the structural skeleton by means of an even façade grid, with sleek translucent panels as infill. The Luxfer Prism Skyscraper, as the project was named, was startling enough to have been called "epoch making" by Henry-Russell Hitchcock in 1942; it surely would have transformed our view of Chicago skyscraper development in the 1890's had it been built. (Not so very different was Willis Polk's Hallidie Building, completed in San Francisco in 1917; its 7-story façade is all of glass, set onto a structural frame and behind ornamental metal cornices. Recently restored, Hallidie remains an extraordinarily prescient building, at once decorative and austere.) Larger in scale were two later skyscraper projects by Wright, a 1920 design for the Press Building in San Francisco, and a 1924 scheme for a building for the National Life Insurance Company in Chicago. The 1920 project set strong vertical elements within a heavy masonry frame topped by a wide cornice; it had touches of Sullivan, but really seemed like Wright's smaller houses blown up to skyscraper scale, though without any of the awkwardness that usually accompanies such shifts. The 1924 project was more innovative: it involved a 27-story structure cantilevered entirely

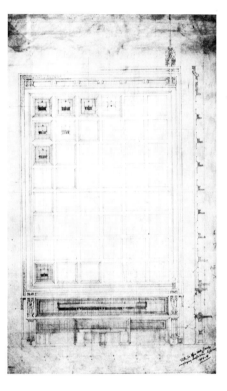

*Elevation for Luxfer Prism skyscraper.
Frank Lloyd Wright, 1895.*

*Opposite: Study by Hugh Ferriss of
skyscraper massing. One of a series
of five drawings.*

49

from central supports, with glass walls hung from the edges of each floor. The building was to have narrow, slablike wings projecting out from a long central slab, a shape as new as the technology that supported it. National Life, as much as Luxfer Prism, would have directed the course of skyscraper history had it been built. Its design stands as another reminder of how innovative Wright was in matters of technology as well as esthetics.

Wright was not alone in considering the possibilities of a skyscraper that would consist largely of glass. In 1921 and 1922, even before National Life's design was completed, Ludwig Mies van der Rohe had proposed two exquisite, stately skyscrapers to be sheathed entirely in glass. They were far more abstract than Wright's: one was to have a prismatic form, the other, a set of curving walls. Mies justified his use of glass by arguing that it, more than any other material, made the quest for structural expressiveness valid: "Skyscrapers reveal their bold structural pattern during construction," he wrote in 1922. "Only then does the gigantic steel web seem impressive. When the outer walls are put in place,

The Hallidie Building, San Francisco. Willis Polk, 1917.

50

the structural system which is the basis of all artistic design is hidden by a chaos of meaningless and trivial forms. When finished, these buildings are impressive only because of their size. . . . Instead of trying to solve the new problems with old forms, we should develop the new forms from the very nature of the new problems."

Mies's views, not to mention his actual forms, foreshadowed concerns that were not to become universal until the second half of the century. "I discovered by working with actual glass models that the important thing is the play of reflections and not the effect of light and shadows as in ordinary buildings," he wrote. And he noted that he had placed the sections of glass wall in the prism skyscraper at slight angles "to avoid the monotony of over-large glass surfaces"—a concern far too few of Mies's followers were to express in times to come.

The skyscraper remained fundamentally an American building type. Throughout the 1920's and beyond, European cities were simply not equipped, for reasons of cultural temperament as much as economy, to build tall. But this made the skyscraper no less interesting to the European avant-garde, who, following Mies's lead, conceived of projects for tall buildings even without the certainty that they would be erected. Indeed, Europeans took considerable advantage of a special opportunity to invent such designs by joining in the remarkable competition sponsored by the Chicago Tribune Company in 1922 to select a design for its new skyscraper home in Chicago.

The competition turned out to be one of the great architectural events of the early part of the century, something of a world's fair of skyscraper design. It surely provided as clear an overview of the state of skyscraper design at that moment in history as anyone could wish for: attracted by the promise of a $50,000 prize and a chance to build a major tower in the heart of Chicago, 260 architects from around the world entered. The competition program summed up the concerns of skyscraper builders and owners in the early 1920's—it called for a building that would symbolize the power and authority of the newspaper, be an efficient operating headquarters, and advance the art of architecture, all at once.

The winners were John Mead Howells and Raymond Hood, whose Gothic tower crowned by a circle of buttresses remains a landmark on North Michigan Avenue. It is a sumptuous, if hardly innovative, scheme: while it lacks the remarkable grace of Woolworth, its proportions are handsome and its overall bearing is self-assured. It is a building that has aged particularly well, and it is hard, looking back after 50 years at the designs that lost to it, to believe that the competition jury made a wrong choice. Their judgment was conservative but sound. Of more impact on architectural history were a number of the losing schemes—though they were not, it now appears, necessarily of higher quality. Most influential was the entry by Eliel Saarinen, which called for a stepped-back central tower, its masses soaring upward like mountains. It won second prize, and the acclaim that surrounded it was such that it led Saarinen to immigrate to the United States. Louis Sullivan wrote a tribute to the Saarinen design, and architects were to imitate it through the decade—even Raymond Hood was to take elements from Saarinen's scheme in some of his later buildings.

The plasticity of Saarinen's design was what attracted most architects to it. It felt sculpted, molded, not constructed, and this seemed to

The Chicago Tribune Tower.
Hood and Howells, 1925.

51

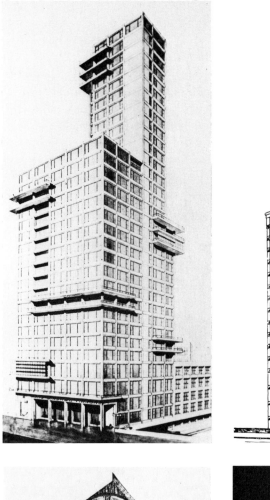

Five losing entries from the Chicago Tribune Competition of 1922. From left to right: Eliel Saarinen (second place), Finland; Walter Gropius and Adolf Meyer, Germany; Heinrich Mossdorf, Germany; Adolf Loos, France; Alfred Fellheimer and Steward Wagner, United States.

70 Pine Street in New York. Rendering
by John Wenrich, 1935.

Overleaf: The New York Tribune
Building. Rendering attributed to
Richard Morris Hunt, 1873.

Portland Public Office Building, park
façade. Rendering by Michael Graves,
1980.

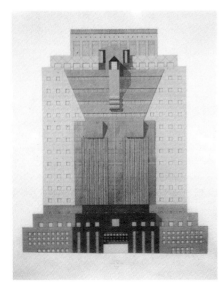

Looking into Madison Square, New York.

Postcards of famous New York buildings. From top: The Metropolitan Life Tower; the Woolworth Building at night; the Flatiron Building.

THE WOOLWORTH BUILDING AND CITY HALL PARK BY NIGHT. NEW YORK CITY.

Fifth Avenue and Flat Iron Building. New York City.

Two paintings of the Shelton Hotel by Georgia O'Keeffe. Right: "New-York Night," 1928–29.

"Shelton with Sun," 1926.

"Chicago," by Louis Lozowick, c. 1923.

"View of Chicago Looking West from Michigan Avenue at the Chicago River," Richard Haas, 1977–78.

The lobby of 2 Park Avenue.

The imported-wood doors of the Chrysler Building's lobby elevators.

Opposite: The lobby of the Empire State Building.

Overleaf: The IDS Building in Minneapolis.

open up a new range of esthetic possibilities. Sullivan, writing from his lonely retirement, called it "a voice, resonant and rich, ringing amidst the wealth and joy of life." Today the Saarinen design, while skillful, seems weaker than the winner—it has a quality of graciousness to it, but not the brilliance and genius ascribed to it. Far more innovative were some of the other European entries—the crisp, sharp scheme of Walter Gropius and Adolph Meyer, at once a Bauhaus experiment and a tribute to the old Chicago skyscraper style; the smooth, rather cool project of Knut Lonberg-Holm, with flat wall planes of different colors prefiguring a concern for sleekness that was to emerge in skyscraper design in later years; the Emerald City vision of the Frenchman J. Batteux, who offered a tower of stripped-down classical masses mounting toward a flamboyant central climax; or the smooth, floating planes of B. Bijvoet and J. Duiker, whose entry from The Netherlands was a refined study in horizontals that, like so much Dutch work of the time, mixed European modernism with the influence of Frank Lloyd Wright. Although a few sought refuge in historical styles, as a group the Dutch and the Germans seemed the most committed to some sort of modernist expression—and, like Gropius and Meyer, tried to merge the concerns of the then-developing European modernist style with the demands of the American skyscraper as a building type.

A number of schemes were intentionally outrageous, such as Heinrich Mossdorf's proposal for a tower topped by the massive head of an Indian, with his tomahawk a kind of light tower, the whole thing a European's smirking view of what American symbolism and ornament should consist of. Adolf Loos's proposal for a skyscraper that would consist essentially of a Doric column was, like Saarinen's, much talked about, if only for its shock value; but as Manfredo Tafuri has pointed out, it appears to have been quite serious. In any event, there were two other schemes that also found a round column a logical solution to the symbolic, freestanding skyscraper.

The Americans tended mostly toward historicism. It is clear that by 1922 the Gothic style had become the accepted mode for the historicist skyscraper; there were twenty Gothic entries from the American contingent, and they tended to be more self-assured than the others, although the general level of quality was higher throughout the American eclectic entries. But there was no shortage of towers with classical temples and Near Eastern domes at the top—it seemed as if architects, far from feeling guilt at the use of historical forms (as Mies, and Sullivan before him, would have urged), were feeling freer than ever. History was like a vast smorgasbord to the American architects of the early 1920's—everything was there for the taking, with visual pleasure the only criterion for choice. It seemed as if the spirit of the New York eclectics, spurned as decadent in Chicago not so many years before, had proved itself the real victor in the Chicago Tribune competition.

The skyscrapers built during these years seemed to bear out the tendency to make the art of composition the real goal. Assembling pieces into a coherent, well-proportioned entity was what skyscraper design had largely become, even in Chicago, where the major skyscraper event preceding the Chicago Tribune competition was the white Wrigley Building of 1921 by Graham, Anderson, Probst, and White, a glistening structure inspired by McKim, Mead, and White's Municipal Building, but with a tower modeled after the Giralda Tower in Seville, Spain. The

The tower of the Wrigley Building, Chicago. Graham, Anderson, Probst, and White, 1921.

proportions are awkward—the tower is gangling, rather like that of
Flagg's Singer Building—but the building surely proved the new direction in which Chicago architecture was headed. More coherent, if drier,
were classicizing buildings like Benjamin Wistar Morris's stately Cu-
nard Building in New York of 1921, or Carrère and Hastings's Standard
Oil Building in New York of 1926, the latter a particularly responsible
and imaginative building urbanistically—it has a curved base,
reflecting the slope of lower Broadway, upon which is set a square tower
aligned with the street grid uptown. So this building responds at once to
the conflicting demands of its immediate surroundings and the skyline of
the city at large. It is monumental, as befits the headquarters of John D.
Rockefeller's enterprises, but it is accommodating, too.

The outright classicism of Standard Oil was to continue to appear
throughout the twenties, but as the decade went on it began gradually to
give way to a somewhat stripped-down, almost sleek, style. The impact
of Saarinen's much-publicized entry in the Chicago Tribune competition, not to mention the growing realization among American architects
of the austere modernist International Style developing in Europe, af-

The Wrigley Building at night.

54

*The Standard Oil Building, New York.
Carrère and Hastings, 1926.*

fected several major works of the second half of the decade. Most notable
was the headquarters building for the New York Telephone Company in
lower Manhattan by Ralph Walker of the firm of Voorhees, Gmelin, and
Walker. Completed in 1926, the Telephone building mounted up sumptuously, with a thick tower rising from a still thicker base amid a wealth
of setbacks. The slenderness and delicacy of the Woolworth was nowhere in evidence, though the detail was lavish and vaguely Gothic. Yet
it was also clearly influenced by the events that had led to the recent Exposition des Arts Décoratifs in Paris: the building's ornate lobby can only
be called Art Deco.

Barclay-Vesey, as the building has also been called—it fills the block
on West Street between Barclay and Vesey streets—is of even greater
significance urbanistically than the Standard Oil Building. As at Stan-

55

The New York Telephone Company Building, also known as the Barclay-Vesey Building, New York. Voorhees, Gmelin, and Walker, 1926.

The legs of this Arts-and-Crafts—style table in the Telephone Building's boardroom represent skyscrapers.

The Telephone Company's bell is the center of the naturalistic ornamentation above the building's main entry.

dard Oil, the tower is square and aligned with the grid of the city, while the base follows the different—in this case parallelogram—shape of the full-block site. The building also has a covered sidewalk arcade along the Vesey Street side, an allusion to the rue de Rivoli that may have been expected to provide an attractive shopping amenity, but that, owing to the building's location away from heavily trafficked areas, never succeeded.

Perhaps most important of all, the building related closely to a celebrated set of studies done by the artist and renderer Hugh Ferriss in response to the provisions of the 1916 zoning ordinance, which, with building booming in the mid-1920's, were only now beginning to be felt. Ferriss's studies, done in association with architect Harvey Wiley Corbett, foresaw buildings rising like mountains, huge masses slicing into the air. In 1922 he produced a set of five drawings indicating what he viewed to be the five stages of development of a design. The series began with an illustration of the total mass available under the zoning law; it was cut away and adjusted gradually in subsequent drawings to admit

57

Four of the series of five Hugh Ferriss drawings showing the massing of skyscrapers possible under New York's 1920 zoning laws. Done in association with Harvey Wiley Corbett, 1922.

light, to create a feasible structure, and to create marketable floors. The series is a progression from a purely abstract mass to a building that, while larger, bears a considerable resemblance to Saarinen's tower or to the Telephone Company building.

Ferriss was one of the great architectural renderers of modern times. His buildings—his renderings of the work of other architects no less than his own imaginative studies—tended to loom like great, sumptuous, dark piles. Ferriss's drawing style became a crucial factor in shaping the priorities of the 1920's: his visions of the impact of the zoning law were to affect the age as much as the law itself, as masonry buildings endeavored to take on the feeling of sculpted mountains, their shape suddenly more important than their historical detail or even their style.

And no building more thoroughly articulated this new tendency toward sculptural mass than the Barclay-Vesey. Walker's building was the object of considerable praise. Lewis Mumford, who had despaired of the American skyscraper's ever breaking out of what he considered to be the morass of historicism ("The mask of American architecture was frozen;

58

the face was dead, the very skyscrapers were born old," he wrote), saw here the dawn of a new age. "One has only to compare the unbroken planes of the Barclay-Vesey Building with the fussiness, the exaggeration of the vertical, the . . . ornamental tricks of the older skyscraper like the Woolworth Tower or the Singer Tower to see the advantages in design."

It was the sense of modernist expression that pleased Mumford— the feeling that the massing of this tower conveyed the idea of its structure. To the moralist Mumford, who had always had leanings toward the Chicago style, this was crucial. "We do not paint pansies on our typewriters or griffons on our automobiles . . . and if we conceived the rest of our environment as freshly as we have conceived these new additions to it, we should strip it similarly to its last essential," Mumford wrote. "To realize form-in-function, by its clear, lucid expression, is what constitutes the modern feeling." Yet the critic's humanist impulse poked through, and he acknowledged that pure structural expression was not enough: "But we are still human beings, not dynamos or Diesel engines, and there must be something more."

Mumford's rather dogmatic view of modernism could not let the Telephone building escape without a few criticisms. He found the intricate, almost naturalistic ornament of the lobby and the lower floors of the exterior—an ornament that was far more literal and less graceful than Sullivan's, but rather overwhelming nonetheless—to be "warm and intimate and a little confused," and he likened it to "a village street in a strawberry festival." What bothered Mumford was the lack of integration between decoration and structure—Walker's ornament seemed applied, not intrinsic to the building, and in this sense it made the Barclay-Vesey, to the orthodox modernist critic at least, less of a real advance over the decorated classical towers than it had appeared to be.

Jazzy Art Deco detail on a corner of 2 Park Avenue.

Today this discrepancy seems less disturbing, and even enlightened—it suggests that Walker was aware of the vastly different roles a lobby interior and an overall structure played, and that he realized that the fulfillment of both of these roles to the greatest degree possible took precedence over any forced and artificial notions of unity. But it is not surprising that back in 1928 Mumford saw as the real harbinger of the new age a far less graceful building, the wide, boxy 2 Park Avenue, built by Ely Jacques Kahn in 1927. This early effort launched Kahn into the position of one of the city's leading architects of Art Deco commercial buildings, much as the Telephone building had done for Ralph Walker. Kahn's huge mass is relieved by a lively, tense array of brightly colored Art Deco detail in terra cotta; it is jazzy more than beautiful, but it sums up the energy of the moment superbly—eager, nervous, dynamic. Kahn went on to do a number of similar buildings throughout Manhattan, including the handsomely massed Squibb Building of 1930, but most of them, like 2 Park Avenue, were of interest more for their spirited detail than for their overall conception.

2 Park Avenue, New York. Ely Jacques Kahn, 1927.

The influence of the Paris Exposition was only beginning to make itself felt in New York in the middle of this vibrant decade, and the factors other than detail that would contribute to the American Art Deco style in the coming years, such as the trend toward streamlining forms, had not yet appeared at all. Just as influential in the mid-twenties were two other Manhattan buildings, both of which had been completed in 1924: Raymond Hood's American Radiator (now American-Standard) Build-

The American Radiator Building (now the American-Standard Building), New York. Raymond Hood, 1924.

"American Radiator." Painting by Georgia O'Keeffe, 1927.

ing on 40th Street opposite Bryant Park, and Arthur Loomis Harmon's Shelton Hotel on Lexington Avenue.

The Radiator Building was a small tower, only 21 stories high, but in it Raymond Hood proved, even more than he had with his partner Howells in their Tribune design, that he could assimilate all of the various influences affecting skyscraper design and produce from them something both coherent and new. The Radiator Building merges Saarinen's Tribune Tower massing with Hood's own Gothic leanings; it is, in a sense, the first- and second-prize winners of the Tribune competition joined in a single building. It is black—Hood's device to make the building seem like a single sculpted mass—and unbroken by windows, which often appear as black holes in lighter buildings. The top is decorated in gold, giving the tower a kind of glowing elegance that prefigured the jazziest skyscrapers of the 1930's. The profile suggests a much larger building; it was Hood's gift that he could create so successful an illusion in massing. He also knew that it was to be placed opposite Bryant Park, where the tower could be seen from a distance.

The American Radiator Building was a remarkable synthesis, an object at once soaring and measured, exuberant and restrained. Arthur Loomis Harmon did not quite have Hood's grace: his Shelton Hotel (now the Halloran House) was entirely sober, with even the Romanesque details at the base and setbacks possessing a certain matter-of-fact air. What was important here was the massing: this was one of the first large towers to be completed under the provisions of the 1916 zoning law, and it became a textbook example, as sure as Hugh Ferriss's renderings, of what the tower of the future would be like. Here, as at Barclay-Vesey, the priority was the sculpting of form, not the making of details. A clay model would have shown the essence of the architect's ideas here far more than an elegantly detailed drawing. But there is considerable power to Harmon's setback tower, and the Shelton's relatively unrelieved masses impressed the city's avant-garde. Georgia O'Keeffe did a series of paintings based on the Shelton's stark forms.

The latter half of the twenties saw a rich array of towers, far more mature, in a sense, than their pre–World War I counterparts. For by this time Chicago's instinct toward structural expression and New York's instinct toward theatricality seemed to have merged. They joined in a series of buildings in these and other cities across the nation that were elegantly, assuredly tall, handsomely massed, and lavishly decorated. Buildings such as Barclay-Vesey and American Radiator led the way for literally dozens of other skyscrapers—so many works of distinction that it is no exaggeration to call the 1920's the richest era in skyscraper design since the early years in Chicago. The buildings of the twenties were looser, more relaxed than their 1880's counterparts; their architects were fundamentally romantic, less concerned with dogma than the early Chicago designers, and they were far more skillful makers of composition than the early New York designers.

The output of this decade, save for obvious icons like Barclay-Vesey and American Radiator, has generally been ignored by architectural historians, in large part because there was little that was really new. Technology had not changed in any substantial way since, say, the Woolworth Building—the skyscraper was still a structure of masonry set on a steel frame—and architects who called for something else, men like Mies van der Rohe and Frank Lloyd Wright, were getting little built. But the

The Shelton Hotel (now the Halloran House), New York. Arthur Loomis Harmon, 1924.

very absence of significant technological developments may well have contributed toward the making of the period's special quality, for designers, freed from grappling with the basic issues of designing for great height, could turn their attention to refining their advances.

As the decade went on, and a rapidly expanding economy led to a constant parade of new skyscrapers, it became increasingly clear that the art of designing tall buildings was, within the limits of the restrictions of zoning and economics, an art of romantic expression. Composition was all: it was the arrangement of masses and the decorative details placed on them that was becoming more important than any choice of style. In other words, whether to build in Gothic or classical was becoming less important; whether to build in a historical style at all was not an issue of deep moral concern to many architects. Their commitment was increasingly to visual pleasure, by any means obtainable.

Hood and his former partner, John Mead Howells, were perhaps the most gifted molders of skyscraper form. Hood had begun to prove his talents as a sole practitioner with the American Radiator Building and would go on to even greater achievements in the 1930's; Howells had to wait until 1928 to show that he too had learned from Saarinen's Chicago Tribune Building, as well as from his own winning scheme. Howells's Panhellenic (now Beekman Tower) Hotel in New York is the American Radiator made sleek with deep vertical reveals, a tiny orange tower pointing the way anxiously toward the crisp lines of the 1930's.

Hood, however, was the greater design talent. Unlike Sullivan or Root, Raymond Hood sought no narrow dogma of skyscraper design; he was an intuitive designer, not a polemicist. But his own lack of ideology, if more frankly admitted than we might expect, is not all that different from the feelings of many of his contemporaries. "My experience, which in reality consists of designing only two skyscrapers: the Tribune and the American Radiator, does not justify my expressing an opinion as to whether a building should be treated vertically, horizontally, or in cubist fashion. On the contrary, it has convinced me that on these matters I should not have a definite opinion. To use these two buildings as examples, they are both in the 'vertical' style or what is called 'Gothic,' simply because I happened to make them so. If at the time of designing them I had been under the spell of Italian campaniles or Chinese pagodas, I suppose the resulting compositions would have been 'horizontal.' . . . Nothing but harm could result if at this stage in our development the free exercise of study and imagination should stop, and the standardizing and formulating of our meager knowledge and experience should now take its place. It might be proper to say something precise about the different styles, but I am as much in the air about style as I am about everything else."

At the end of the twenties, the compositions seemed to get madder, wilder in every way. Curlett and Beelman's 1926 Elks Club in Los Angeles is a sort of Mayan composition with Romanesque and Gothic details. The sculpture seems to grow out of it, almost oozing from the stonework. Similar, but far better in every aspect of its conception, were a pair of towers designed by Bertram Grosvenor Goodhue, the Gothicist who began an earnest search in the 1920's for a style that would somehow merge his historicist leanings with the modernist impulse. Goodhue proposed an immense tower for Madison Square in New York that, had it been built, would clearly have been among the city's most remarkable skyscrapers: it shot straight up from a 20-story base that was itself a skillful

Madison Square Tower Project, New York. Bertram Grosvenor Goodhue.

Opposite: The Panhellenic Hotel (now the Beekman Tower Hotel), New York. John Mead Howells, 1928.

63

Nebraska State Capitol, Lincoln.
Bertram Grosvenor Goodhue, 1932.

study in setback. A vast arched entrance was scaled to the huge size of the project; the tower was to rise sheer for most of its height, with gradual setbacks near the top and an ornate spire.

The tower was inventive in its uses: it was to contain a church in its base, with offices above. The detail was vaguely Gothic, but with a smoothness to it that suggested that Eliel Saarinen's Chicago Tribune scheme had not gone unnoticed by Goodhue either. There is a power to this skyscraper design that has seldom been equaled: thanks to its four solid corner piers, the building seemed not merely covered with stone, but absolutely molded from it, carved out of solid rock.

The building's solid corners would have prevented any corner offices, a serious rental liability. No such marketing realities were an issue with the Goodhue tower that did get built, the Nebraska State Capitol at Lincoln. Here, a similar tower rose from a much broader, more classicizing base—this is the skyscraper over the base of a civic monument as opposed to the skyscraper over the base of another skyscraper, as Madison Square would have been. The tower here is smaller, and culminates in a golden, almost Byzantine dome, but the conception is not dissimilar from Madison Square. Once again, one senses Goodhue's brilliance at handling masses, at molding a whole building like a plastic sculpture—a gift evident as far back as the early years of the twentieth century, when he designed striking and original Gothic churches. Indeed, Goodhue's desire here was to do a building that would not bear any clear resemblance to any historical style at all but would instead be an exercise in pure form and texture and shadow.

Nebraska is a symbolic tower more than a true skyscraper—Goodhue had intended it to stand out as a vertical mark on the plains, and did not even plan to place offices in the building's high section. Later, the state government did so, turning the building into a more conventionally used skyscraper. Its construction spanned an entire decade, from 1922 to 1932; the design had come two years earlier, as the result of a competition. So the building, as an idea at least, really opened the twenties. Goodhue's models were Scandinavian and German church architecture more than existing skyscrapers—what he had done was not merely to turn the American commercial skyscraper into a public building but to broaden the range of sources for that building, to carry it into abstract forms in a way no American architect had heretofore been able to do. Goodhue died in 1924, long before the building was completed. He was 54; it is impossible to know what influence he might have had on skyscraper design had he lived. But it is worth observing here how popular the Nebraska State Capitol has always been, despite its break with both the tradition of state capitols and the development of American skyscraper design. A local businessman wrote in a letter to the State Capitol Commission after Goodhue's winning design was announced: "I love this new building. There is something fascinating about the whole thing. It seems to grow on one. It sounds depths in us that we never knew existed before. Everyone seems to be inspired by its presence. I hope the reality will be as great."

Nothing else precisely like Goodhue's buildings was built in the twenties, but there were a few towers that might be called Goodhue-esque. C. Howard Crane's 46-story American Insurance Union Citadel of 1927, in Columbus, Ohio, rose in powerful verticals to an octagonal

American Insurance Union Citadel, Columbus, Ohio. C. Howard Crane, 1927.

tower topped by a domelike crown; elaborate sculpture grew out of its uppermost corners, and the building probably comes closer to giving us a sense of what Goodhue's Madison Square skyscraper would have looked like than any other completed building. Like Goodhue's towers, the American Insurance is at once sleekly modern and heavily Byzantine, possessing the air of a civic monument more than that of an office building. The same might be said of the 30-story Los Angeles City Hall, completed in 1928, designed by John C. Austin, John Parkinson, and Albert C. Martin; here again a certain Mayan massing merged with classical details and a pyramidal top to create a monumental tower, for more than a generation the only very tall building in Los Angeles. More graceful, if more admittedly historicist, was the Williamsburgh Savings Bank Tower of 1929, in Brooklyn, by Halsey, McCormick, and Helmer, a strongly Romanesque tower rising to 36 stories and topped off by a round dome—à la Goodhue—and by a massive four-sided clock, each of whose faces measures 27 feet in diameter. The Williamsburgh was erected at the intersection of Atlantic and Flatbush avenues, near the Long Island Railroad Terminal; every planning precept would have suggested that its corner was the logical commercial center for the borough, and the bank, with its tall tower rising atop an unusually lavish Romanesque banking room, was prepared to stake out the territory first. But nothing ever followed, and the tower stands now, half a century later, rather mournfully amid a mé-

City Hall, Los Angeles. Austin, Parkinson, and Martin, 1928.

The Williamsburgh clock tower.

67

lange of small businesses in ramshackle structures. It would be a startling context for a skyscraper in any city, but it is even more so in New York, where tall buildings are so crowded by their equals.

Rounded and pyramidal tops were by no means the only favored skyscraper crowns in the second half of the decade. For the 1926 Paramount Building in Times Square in New York, Rapp and Rapp produced a 19-foot-wide glass globe set atop a structure so frequently set back that its overall mass resembled a pyramid. Schultze and Weaver Gothicized the top of the slender Sherry-Netherland Hotel of 1927, in New York; Emery Roth set a pair of classical peristyle tempietti atop the San Remo Apartments, in New York, not completed until 1930—both articulate reminders that a pure historicism had not disappeared at all. Irwin Chanin was more modern, or at least *moderne,* in his Majestic and Cen-

The Fuller Building, New York.
Walker and Gillette, 1929.

The Art Deco lintel above the entryway
to the Fuller Building.

Opposite: The Fred French Building,
New York. Fred F. French Company;
Sloan and Robertson, 1927.

tury Apartments of 1930 and 1931, twin-towered buildings with jazz deco tops. Not so different was Walker and Gillette's Fuller Building of 1929, to which the Fuller Construction Company moved from the Flatiron building. This time the company permitted no bizarre shape that would replace its own name in the public mind, as Flatiron had done; the new Fuller Building is a slender tower of white brick, its top a series of setbacks in black and white masonry that looks rather like an Art Deco version of an Aztec temple. Sloan and Robertson, on the other hand, chose pure decoration in 1927 for the crown of the Fred F. French Building in New York: a tower whose massing was determined largely by zoning laws, but which stood out from its neighbors boldly by virtue of its extravagant sunburst mosaic top. The French Building actually has a flat roof, a precursor of slabs to come; the decoration is in fact a pair of huge panels set into the top of the slab like great signs.

As the decade ended, the greatest skyscrapers of the thirties were in design and, in some cases, already in construction, and there had been a few major towers just completed that seemed especially to look forward to the new decade. But the preoccupations of the twenties seem best summarized by a trio of buildings that looked backward, not forward, to a kind of splashy, if conservative, historicism, yet were impressive works of urban planning—the General Electric Building (originally the RCA Building) in New York, by Cross and Cross; the New York Central Building (now the Helmsley Building) in New York, by Warren and Wetmore; and the Terminal Tower in Cleveland, by Graham, Anderson, Probst, and White. The New York Central Building was finished in 1929, the Cleveland tower and the General Electric building just after the turn of the decade, in 1931.

The General Electric Building is a slender tower, 51 stories high; as a building it has much in common with many of the New York skyscrapers of the twenties. Two things distinguish it: the ornate stone tracery of the crown and the relationship of the building to St. Bartholomew's

The General Electric Building (originally the RCA Building), New York. Cross and Cross, 1931.

The lobby of the General Electric Building.

72

Church, the distinguished Goodhue building it abuts. The tower top was intended to suggest radio waves, and indeed it does so, or at least the physical image of radio waves as it existed in the public imagination in the days of that medium's youth; what is remarkable is how much the crown also suggests traditional Gothic spires, and how little contradiction one feels between these two things. Cross and Cross gracefully joined two distinct sets of images—that of twentieth-century technology and that of medieval architecture—and though their methods were less subtle than those of Cass Gilbert at Woolworth, the results were almost as admirable.

As important, surely, as General Electric's spire is the ease with which it recedes into the background behind St. Bartholomew's. Cross and Cross chose for their Lexington Avenue building only materials and colors that were compatible with Goodhue's church on Park Avenue, and the result is a cogent response to any suggestion that a 51-story tower and a low church cannot coexist. They can indeed, and if Cross and Cross's crown shows the preoccupation of the 1920's with fanciful image-making, the building as a whole prefigures the importance architects were to give to urban relationships decades later. (It also inspired in 1980 a responsible, if dull, smaller brick skyscraper by the Eggers Group next door, on a site that also abuts the church.)

The construction around Grand Central Terminal in New York, which went into high gear after the completion of the terminal in 1913, was an early and impressive example of sophisticated urbanism—buildings were seen as parts of a greater whole, not as isolated objects in themselves. The New York Central Railroad owned all the land around the terminal, and thus could exercise far more control than the average builder. The railroad was, in fact, one of the most powerful real estate developers in New York City. Most of the buildings erected on its land—the Biltmore Hotel, by Warren and Wetmore, of 1914, for example—were relatively staid, classically detailed masses, whose chief virtue was a certain somber compatibility. In the railroad's own headquarters, however, Warren and Wetmore achieved a building of energetic, lavish style, and did so not only without compromise to the integrity of the overall group, but with enhancement of it.

The New York Central Building sits squat in the center of Park Avenue, terminating a vista from miles north and, until the Pan Am Building blocked its southern side, for miles south as well. The tower's overall

73

form is perfect for its unusual site—an ornate pyramidal crown topped by a cupola acts as an anchor, almost an exclamation point, in the center of Park Avenue. Once there was an even, or relatively even, cornice line going all the way up Park Avenue, making the New York Central the conductor of a two-mile urbanistic ensemble; that order has now turned to disarray, but the building's overall quality is not diminished. The tower's accommodating relationship to what surrounded it was not limited to its shape: the building also contains two great arches through which the automobile traffic of Park Avenue passes.

The building was recently restored by its present owner, the real estate developer Harry Helmsley (it had gone through a period of ownership by the Kennedy family after the railroad sold it), who renamed it the Helmsley Building. The elaborate lobby, a veritable ballroom in the midst of Park Avenue, has been cleaned, and the façade has been given so much gilt that it resembles a woman with a bit too much makeup. But the top is floodlit, and this has given the tower's flamboyant crown even greater symbolic power.

Cleveland's building is less successful esthetically—it was designed by the architects, descended from Daniel Burnham's firm, who had given New York its vast Equitable Building—and its ornate classical top comes almost directly off McKim, Mead, and White's Municipal Building of 17 years before. But Terminal Tower, like the New York Central Building, represented an emerging sense that a skyscraper was part of an interlocking urban system, and here the system merged eloquently with a higher tower to create a building that was at once civic symbol and urban workhorse. Terminal Tower contained, in addition to a 700-foot, 52-story office wing, a train station, a rapid transit station, a department store, restaurants, banks, smaller office wings, and a hotel (part of which was renovated from an existing building on the site). The commercial wings were constructed on air rights over the tracks, as the buildings around Grand Central in New York had been; here, of course, the city is so much smaller that the terminal complex functions as a clearly visible symbol, as obvious a rallying point as any church tower of old. So Terminal Tower controlled its city's skyline, yet it wove itself into the fabric of the city at the same time. It was something few skyscrapers in any city have managed to do, at any point in history.

The clock above the New York Central Building. Edward McCartan, sculptor.

Opposite: New York Central Building (now the Helmsley Building). Warren and Wetmore, 1929.

75

CHAPTER FIVE
THE DRIVE FOR HEIGHT

If a kind of free-form eclecticism, a merging of the forms of architectural history in an increasingly loose way, could be considered the preoccupation of the 1920's, skyscraper design in the 1930's jelled into something more coherent. There was a clear priority in the new decade: height. In 1930 the Woolworth had been the world's tallest building for 17 years, its position so venerable for many of those years that even to propose to top it would have seemed vulgar and disrespectful, like suggesting a structure for Washington, D.C., that would climb higher than the Washington Monument.

Not that there hadn't been plans for taller buildings. In 1926 John Larkin, a New York architect and engineer, announced a plan to erect a 110-story skyscraper on West 42nd Street between Eighth and Ninth avenues in Manhattan—the site that not many years later was to be occupied by the McGraw-Hill Building, Raymond Hood's masterpiece of the early 1930's. Larkin's building was to rise 1,208 feet above the sidewalk, making it the first building to surpass the height of the Eiffel Tower, which had remained the tallest structure in the world. The Larkin Tower, as the project was known, was a design of startling banality—it had a base of setbacks, atop which rose a square brick tower that narrowed several times toward the top, like the sections of a telescope. It looked almost like a child's version of a skyscraper, and given the considerable inventiveness of the buildings that were actually being constructed in the late 1920's, it is not surprising that the scheme was greeted with some skepticism.

Many of the doubts centered on technical and not esthetic issues, however. Larkin was challenged by builders and architects on his steel frame structural system, which many critics felt could not support so tall a tower, and on the elevators, which he designed as double-deck cars, intending to reduce the number of elevator shafts necessary. Elevators were a serious design problem, as much a limit to height as any technological restrictions could be: when a building reached extreme heights, so many elevators were required that large amounts of floor space in the lower floors had to be given over to elevator shafts. There was a point at which greater height produced not more rentable floor space but less, so intrusive were the demands of vertical transportation.

Larkin Tower. Design by John Larkin, New York, 1926.

Opposite: Three Manhattan towers: the General Electric is on the left; the Chrysler is in the center; and one of the Waldorf-Astoria Hotel's twin towers is on the right.

Irwin Chanin's private bath, an ornate Art Deco fantasy in the Chanin Building.

The Chanin Building, New York. Sloan and Robertson, 1929.

Larkin's slender tower could not have been particularly economical—the upper floors would have been tiny, aeries with glorious views and natural light but with barely adequate space for even small business enterprises. Small tower floors were to a certain extent the inevitable result of any design based on setbacks, but Larkin's building seemed to lack large amounts of floor space for virtually its entire height. Whether it was economic or design problems that put an end to the Larkin scheme is irrelevant now, of course, but it should be remembered that it was not many years later that buildings very like the Larkin Tower were not only designed but built.

The drive for height led to a number of significant Manhattan towers in the late 1920's and early 1930's. Sloan and Robertson's Chanin Building, finished in 1929 for the architect and developer Irwin Chanin, was the first: just under the Woolworth Building in height (680 feet to Woolworth's 792), it nevertheless had more floors, and its prominence in midtown Manhattan—it is on the southwest corner of 42nd Street and Lexington Avenue—seemed to suggest that not only was a new building rivaling Woolworth in height, but an entire new neighborhood, midtown Manhattan, was coming into its own. Chanin's design was loosely based on the Saarinen scheme for the Chicago Tribune, as were so many notable towers of the period, but here Saarinen's squarish tower is stretched into a slender slab, and the architects gave Chanin an explosion of Art Deco detailing, with ornate bas-reliefs in terra cotta around the base and elaborately sculpted brass grillwork in the lobby. Up on the executive floor, Irwin Chanin's private bath is a fantasy of Art Deco tile work.

The Chanin Building was to have only a brief moment of dominance in midtown Manhattan. It was quickly followed by a skyscraper that overtook Woolworth and the Eiffel Tower as well, a tower that rose just across the street at the northeast corner of 42nd and Lexington—the Chrysler Building, designed by William Van Alen and completed in 1930.

Chrysler rose to 1,048 feet, and at 77 stories it was clearly the world's tallest building. It would have been notable even at a lesser height, however, for Van Alen's design was like that of no skyscraper that had come

A scene from the "Skyline of New York" ballet at the 1931 Beaux Arts Ball at the Astor Hotel. The theme was a "Fête Moderne," and the architects are dressed as their skyscrapers. From left to right: A. Stewart Walker, the Fuller Building; Leonard Schultze, the Waldorf-Astoria Hotel; Ely Jacques Kahn, the Squibb Building; William Van Alen, the Chrysler Building; Ralph Walker, Number 1 Wall Street; D. E. Ward, the Metropolitan Life Tower; J. H. Freedlander, the Museum of the City of New York.

Two early studies for the Chrysler Building.

before. The tower was of white brick, with gray brick ornamental trim and gargoyles fashioned after 1929 Chrysler automobile hood ornaments; it culminated in a series of stainless-steel arches punctured by triangular windows and culminating in a great spire. The lobby was finished in deep red African marble, and the paneled elevator cabs were each finished in a different pattern of wood inlays. The building has been called Art Deco, and it surely echoes the spirit of the *moderne* that had been growing in popularity since the mid-1920's, but Chrysler goes beyond Art Deco to become a truly new kind of skyscraper. Its bizarre form seems a perfect encapsulation of the energy and flamboyance of Manhattan at the end of the 1920's—all of the drive for height, all of the theatrical passion seem expressed in those flashy arches and slender spire. Chrysler's romanticism is a far more appropriate statement of what New York wanted to be about as the twenties turned into the thirties than any historicist skyscraper or International Style box. Yet for all its strangeness, it is never *too* strange—the quality of Chrysler as a work of architecture comes from its ability to be romantic and irrational and yet not quite so foolish as to be laughable; it stops just short and retains credibility in the midst of fantasy.

It is no surprise, then, that Chrysler has been a beloved symbol of New York for half a century—it is the sort of building that seems to encourage an emotional response more than an intellectual one. It was disliked by most architects when it was new—Kenneth Franzheim called Van Alen "the Ziegfeld of his profession"—but it has weathered the cycles of taste with more success than almost any other major tower. Chrysler's form, it should be noted, was the final of several versions,

The Chrysler Building in its final form: New York. William Van Alen, 1930.

none of which was as good as what was built. As originally conceived by Van Alen, the skyscraper would have had a more rounded top, giving it a faintly Byzantine or Moorish air, an awkward finish indeed for the sleek, jazz-modern base.

The spire, too, was not part of the original scheme, and it came about as a result of one of the most intense rivalries of the period. As Chrysler was under construction, Van Alen's former partner, H. Craig Severance with his partner Yasuo Matsui, was completing a 66-story skyscraper at 40 Wall Street topped by an ornate pyramidal crown, not unlike that of the New York Central Building. Chrysler's originally announced height was 925 feet, and 40 Wall Street, the headquarters of the Bank of The Manhattan Company, was set to top off at 927 feet, making it the tallest building in the world. Van Alen was determined that Chrysler should

The Chrysler top of stainless steel arches punctuated with triangular windows.

40 Wall Street, New York. H. Craig Severance and Yasuo Matsui, 1930. Pencil sketch by Hugh Ferriss, c. 1929.

*Margaret Bourke-White takes a
photograph from one of the Chrysler
Building's gargoyles.*

have the title, so he added the spire, which was secretly assembled
within Chrysler's crown and raised into place just as the tower was finished, leaving Severance in a distant second place.

The event itself epitomized the craze for height that gripped architects and builders at the turn of the decade. Severance's building, which
did manage to command the lower Manhattan skyline with considerable
grandeur despite its snub by Chrysler, was itself nearly equaled in 1932
by a neighbor, Clinton and Russell's Cities Services Building at 70 Pine
Street (also known as 60 Wall Tower), a brick Art Deco tower of 66 stories culminating in an ornate setback crown complete with Art Deco so-
larium and softly glowing lights. It is one of the New York skyline's finest
tops—more an echo of the jazz age life of midtown Manhattan, in fact,
than of the corporate life of the downtown financial district of which it is
a part.

But all of the passion and inventiveness that Van Alen invested in his
drive to achieve the "world's tallest" record for Chrysler proved of little
lasting value. Even before Chrysler had reached its full height, construction was under way on another tower which would render it modest
by comparison and bring John Larkin's dream of a tower of more than
100 floors to realization at last. It was the Empire State Building, on the
site of the old Waldorf-Astoria Hotel on 34th Street at Fifth Avenue; the

The Empire State Building, New York.
Shreve, Lamb, and Harmon, 1931.

designs of architects Shreve, Lamb, and Harmon would bring it to 102 stories and 1,250 feet.

The Empire State was a purely speculative venture, more like the Equitable Building of 1915 than the Chrysler Building, which was so much a personal project of the automobile magnate Walter P. Chrysler. The Empire State was backed by John J. Raskob and Pierre S. du Pont, with former Governor Alfred E. Smith as their front man; they wanted something big, not necessarily something distinctive, and it is only a matter of luck that William F. Lamb came up with so excellent a design. Lamb was known mostly for efficient, straightforward commercial designs, and he conceived the Empire State tower as the simplest way of applying existing zoning laws. What emerged, however, was an immensely skillful piece of massing—a 5-story base, filling out the full site, above which rises a tower with its mass correctly broken by indentations running the full height, and topped off by a crown of setbacks culminating in a gently rounded tower.

If it is not quite as inventive a profile as that of the Chrysler Building, it is more restrained and dignified, and just as handsome. The limestone, granite, aluminum, and nickel of the façade create a streamlined, grayish tone that is appropriate both for New York and for the idea of height, and there is just the right hint of Art Deco ornament. The 5-story base, for its part, holds the street line well and assures that the huge hulk of the tower is at a soft visual and psychological distance from passersby. It has been criticized as difficult to see from nearby, which indeed it is, but this is as much the fault of the Manhattan street grid as of anything else, for there are no open spaces from which to view any towers in New York in their full height. The Empire State is best seen from afar, where its tower seems at once to blend into the skyline and to command it.

The Empire State, even more than the Chrysler Building, became a symbol not only of the New York skyline, but of tall buildings everywhere. It became for the 1930's what the Woolworth Building had been

Lightning striking the Empire State tower.

King Kong atop the Empire State Building.

85

earlier in the century—a natural wonder as much as a building, a phenomenon that would enter the popular lore. It was startling, but somehow not all that surprising. Then in 1945, ten years after the building had been completed, a small plane flying off course in a Saturday morning fog rammed into the 76th floor, and suddenly this tower seemed to many people to be higher than God may have intended buildings to be. (The pilot was killed, and so were 13 other people, but there were not many other injuries, since there were few people in the building on the day of the accident.) That the tower sustained little structural damage—despite the fact that the plane flew right into an outside wall—the building's owners took as a sign of the Empire State's durability.

The completion of the Empire State and Chrysler buildings, not to mention all the tall towers downtown, effectively answered any questions about the economic viability of skyscrapers: if they had not been able to make money, these vast buildings would not have been built. Still, the Empire State Building, which opened in the midst of the Depression, rented so slowly that for years it was referred to as the "Empty State Building." But unlike some kinds of skyscrapers, it *could* make money once it was amply rented. A study for the American Institute of Steel Construction in 1929 reported that the optimum height for a building on a midtown Manhattan site would be about 63 stories—at that height, enough income would be produced to offset the high cost of land in central business districts (a cost made higher, of course, by the feasibility of erecting huge skyscrapers on these sites), yet there were not so many floors that the number of elevators required would cut sharply into available rental space in lower floors. The study showed diminishing returns at greater height, until at 132 stories it projected that profits would disappear altogether.

As both the size and the number of skyscrapers in all American cities, not merely New York, grew, the debate over the sense such large

The Empire State immediately became a symbol of Manhattan. This view, looking toward the harbor from midtown, is one of the best-known shots of New York.

A romanticized portrait of the Empire State's tower in the clouds. By Charlotte Price, 1950.

buildings made surfaced again. The controversy of the early years of the century had never fully died away—it had merely ebbed, been rendered somewhat irrelevant by the insistent presence of huge buildings in virtually every downtown business district. Now, however, the truly vast size of the new generation of skyscrapers seemed to make certain questions valid again. Did it make sense to build so tall? Was it the best thing esthetically for cities, even if it could be justified economically? Should tall buildings be allowed to cluster together, or should they be kept wide apart, guaranteeing light and air for everyone in each tower?

Of the answer to that last question Frank Lloyd Wright was particularly certain. He rejected the gathering of skyscrapers in business districts as a violation of the essential spirit of any tower, and cared little about the forces of the real estate market that would be thrown asunder by a system that would permit skyscrapers on one block and not on a site a block away. For Wright really objected to the dense core city in its very essence—he was violently antiurban; his ideal skyscraper was not a city building at all, but a tower in the open countryside. He proposed such buildings frequently, although his most famous skyscraper was in fact an urban building—a mile-high tower planned in 1956 for Chicago. It was a typically Wrightian gesture—bold, sweeping, at once seeming to mock the skyscraper frenzy of the late 1920's and to carry it to a new level.

87

But it was not only Frank Lloyd Wright who feared that skyscrapers were leading to a madly overbuilt, unworkably dense city. Thomas Alva Edison, the inventor, said in a 1926 interview, quoted in *Literary Digest,* "If . . . New York keeps on permitting the building of skyscrapers, each one having as many people every day as we used to have in a small city, disaster must overtake us. When all of the people in those skyscrapers start to flow out into the street at approximately the same moment or within a half-hour or an hour, try to get to the entrances of those buildings so that they may begin the day's business, there must be such overcrowding of the streets near those skyscrapers as must stop traffic."

Others agreed. Thomas Hastings, who had been raising doubts about the skyscraper since before the turn of the century, was particularly alarmed at the new proliferation. "We shall experience the greatest calamity that has ever befallen a municipality," Hastings warned in a 1927 essay, "The City of Dreadful Height," in which he decried the rapidly increasing density of Manhattan. "It is a matter of justice and sanitation and circulation and not a matter of art," Hastings said. "It is rather for the protection of the small property owner, to save him from the encroachment upon his rights, which robs him of light and air and at the same time robs those in other neighborhoods of that increased valuation of their property which would be occasioned by the increased demand in his neighborhood if we were obliged to spread out instead of building up in the air."

Scientific American, the *Literary Digest,* and the *Atlantic* seemed to be leading the crusade in the popular press for some sort of limits to skyscraper construction; *Scientific American'*s writers in particular seemed concerned, as Edison had been, about traffic congestion emanating from skyscraper construction. But that argument was refuted by Harvey Wiley Corbett, the New York architect who was to become one of the skyscraper's most articulate defenders, who claimed that skyscrapers in fact reduced traffic by clustering businesses close together and obviating the need for various automobile trips. London's traffic problems are worse than New York's, Corbett pointed out, and yet there are no skyscrapers at all in that city, where business functions are spread over a vast area. Corbett believed the solution lay not in a reduction of skyscrapers,

One of Harvey Wiley Corbett's schemes for double-layered streets to help with traffic congestion in Manhattan. Drawn by Hugh Ferriss.

Frank Lloyd Wright reveals the design for his Mile-High Skyscraper in Chicago, 1956.

but in a greater order to the vast new city, and he proposed a number of schemes for double-layered streets, with motor traffic in a covered lower level and pedestrians on an open upper level. Corbett's street designs were drawn up by Hugh Ferriss, the great renderer and theorist of the new sky-scraper, and they remained in the public eye for years—though no move was ever made to bring them to fruition.

Corbett's view that salvation came not by eliminating skyscrapers but by bringing to them a greater order was shared by another major theorist of twentieth-century urban order, Le Corbusier. The French-Swiss architect's comment on his first visit to New York, which shocked the city's architectural community, is by now well-known: "The sky-scrapers of New York are too small and there are too many of them." What Le Corbusier sought was a more rational city, a city that could be understood and predicted, a city whose architecture would be as ordered as its Cartesian street grid.

Could it ever be so? One of the things the critics of the great burst of skyscraper construction were grappling with was a feeling that the city

Part of the romance of the Empire State was in its construction. Lewis Hine took a series of photographs that have become classics.

could not, in fact, be tamed. There had always been a certain sense of anarchy to New York's physical makeup; the wild and energetic historical cribbings of the city's early skyscrapers were proof of that. But the huge towers of the late twenties and early thirties seemed to move the city to a whole other level, to a scale at which the lack of order became more threatening, more disturbing, than it had been before. The possibilities for height seemed limitless and so did the possibilities for growth—and therefore, to many, so were the possibilities for overbuilding, for chaos, for catastrophe. There were predictions in the journals of the day of cities so full of towers that their skyline had become just a single mass, their streets a mob of pedestrians, the sky invisible, fresh air and views forgotten amenities. It was no longer the romance of "King's Dream" but a fear of a congestion far greater, with none of the fresh new energy of the first wave of skyscraper building. In such a climate it is no surprise that the calls to order of Le Corbusier, Harvey Corbett, Edison, and others could carry such weight. They were like prophets, exhorting the builders of skyscrapers to repent of their sins.

The critics of skyscrapers at this time carried a certain moral authority, but their words still rang somewhat hollow. For the evidence in the late 1920's was clearly that skyscrapers did not destroy cities; they made them look different, and they made their sidewalks more crowded, but they did not put an end to healthy urban civilization at all. In the earlier skyscraper debates there had been little real evidence, for not much had been built; but by this time the evidence was everywhere. What the critics of the 1920's lacked was a coherent sense of what a complex organism the city really was. Each of them offered a different solution—Le Corbusier wanted to change the city into a set of rigid, widely separated towers in open space, Wright wanted to demolish the city altogether, Corbett wanted to create rational transportation systems—but in each case there was an assumption that a rational structure could be created to solve all problems. Physical order could be imposed, and with it, each critic asserted, all problems would recede.

It was Raymond Hood, the great architect of early twenties skyscrapers, who appeared to see the situation in clearer perspective. "Congestion is good," Hood said. "New York is the first place in the world where

Building the Empire State.

90

"The Sky-boy," showing a worker ascending a cable with the Hudson River in the background, is perhaps the most famous of the Hine series.

a man can work within a ten-minute walk of a quarter of a million peo-ple. . . . Think how this expands the field from which we can choose our friends, our co-workers and contacts, how easy it is to develop a con-stant interchange of thought."

To Hood, the city was a marketplace of ideas, a place to which the very idea of congestion was basic—not a barrier to its correct function-ing but an enhancement of it. The anarchic city of skyscrapers was not so disturbing: so long as congestion was kept within reason, it could in fact be a catalyst to an enlivened city, Hood thought. It is a view that time has borne out—that the cities or neighborhoods based on the Corbu-sieran model have been, for the most part, banal failures is rarely dis-puted today—but in the 1930's, the suggestion that the vitality of the city might be a result of its physical density and disorder, rather than something that existed in spite of these characteristics, must have seemed radical indeed.

Hood's realization that the city was not an easily rationalized object was not meant to be a license to permit it to grow wildly; as his later work on the planning team of Rockefeller Center showed, Hood deeply re-spected certain kinds of formal order. But he also recognized fundamen-tal facts about cities and about the role skyscrapers might play in them that would not be widely understood or appreciated for at least another generation. In the early thirties, when density and exuberant growth were praised, it was generally by boosters, not planners—in paeans to the skyline like the promotional book *New York: The Wonder City,* pub-lished in 1932, which listed every skyscraper in town on a page of its own, describing most as the biggest or the grandest or the most luxurious ever built, and began with the sentence, "New York—synonym for big, great, astounding, miraculous! New York—mecca which lures the brightest minds, the most brilliant writers, the most masterful artisans to its gates! New York—what visions of magnitude, variety and power the name New York conjures up for human comprehension!" Most serious minds dismissed such rhetoric as claptrap; it was Hood's gift to see beyond the hyperbole and recognize that within the cliché lay a basic truth.

Chryzler Bldg & Other Skyscrap
Copyright 1930 by Irving Underhill
N.Y.C.

CHAPTER SIX

RHYTHMS OF THE THIRTIES

Raymond Hood remains a curious figure—the most graceful molder of the skyscraper form throughout the 1920's, much of his best work was based on the designs of another architect, Eliel Saarinen. A man who achieved fame through a Gothic-style tower—the Chicago Tribune Building—he spent the rest of his career moving away from revivalism. And though he celebrated the congestion and romance of the city, he designed several rigorously ordered buildings that are considered among the finest International Style skyscrapers in the United States.

The first major Hood work in New York after the American Radiator Building was the new headquarters for the New York *Daily News* at 220 East 42nd Street, completed in 1930. There is no mystery as to how Hood got this commission: the tabloid *News* was started by the Chicago Tribune Company, whose owners were still so pleased with Hood's work that they could not have conceived of offering the job to another architect.

But if they were expecting another Gothic extravaganza, they were surprised: Hood (along with John Mead Howells, with whom he was again associated for this project) produced a building that broke forcefully with the line of skyscraper development of the previous decade. The elaborate setbacks culminating in an ornamental crown were gone, and in their place was a relatively simple slab, made up of white brick verticals giving a sharp and crisp sense of height, within which were set recessed lines of windows and spandrels. There are setbacks, but they are carefully positioned to enhance the sense of pure height and provide just a hint of relief from the stark form.

The building is cool and controlled in a way that none of the flamboyant towers of the 1920's had been. There is a smoothness here, and a sense of an upward driving force, that, for 1930, must have seemed remarkably daring—it is no surprise that compared to the Daily News, Chrysler seemed overblown and showy to the avant-garde. But the Daily News is far from a stark slab of the sort that would become common after World War II; there are sculpted red and black brick spandrels to provide some relief, and the ornate sculpted bas-relief over the front door is particularly rich, a decorative detail that foreshadowed Hood's later work at Rockefeller Center.

Opposite: View of midtown Manhattan in 1930. In the foreground is 295 Madison Avenue (Charles F. Moyer Company, 1929) and the Lincoln Building (J. E. R. Carpenter, 1930); the Chanin and Chrysler buildings are in midview; the Daily News is behind.

93

The Daily News Building, New York.
Raymond Hood, 1930.

The lobby of the Daily News Building.

It was just two years later that Hood, this time with partner André Fouilhoux, switched gears again to create a building that, for shock value at least, made an even greater mark than the Daily News Building—the McGraw-Hill Building at 330 West 42nd Street, on the very site that John Larkin had selected in 1926 for his 110-story tower. McGraw-Hill is sheathed in a greenish-turquoise terra cotta, and its setback form culminates in an ornate, jazz-modern signboard. Vincent Scully called it "proto-jukebox," which comes as close to an accurate description as anything else, although it ignores the rather severe, industrial aspects of the body of the structure. McGraw-Hill is far brasher and livelier than Daily News, yet it was the only New York skyscraper selected by Henry-Russell Hitchcock and Philip Johnson for inclusion in *The International Style,* their 1932 anthology of buildings that seemed in accord with the rigid tenets of academic European modernism. It was the factorylike aspect of much of the building that earned the respect of the International Style polemicists of the 1930's: "The McGraw-Hill Building comes nearest to achieving esthetically the expression of the enclosed steel cage," Hitchcock and Johnson wrote.

If McGraw-Hill is somewhat showy—it is the only skyscraper of impeccable modernist credentials that is as much fun to look at as the Chrysler Building—its opposite number was surely the headquarters

Opposite: The McGraw-Hill Building,
New York. Raymond Hood, 1932.

94

95

The letters of the Philadelphia Saving Fund Society became part of the building's design.

for the Philadelphia Saving Fund Society, by George Howe and William Lescaze, completed in the same year, 1932. This building was no casual essay in modernism by a brilliant compositionalist, as was Hood's effort, but an absolutely serious attempt to evolve a new skyscraper form in accord with the guidelines of the International Style. Howe was an established Philadelphia architect who was coming to tire of picturesque romanticism and was seeking a style of more intellectual rigor; Lescaze was a European modernist, and together they made a brilliant, if unorthodox, team.

The building is as earnest a modern skyscraper as the United States was to see until after World War II. All of the hallmarks of the International Style were there—horizontal strip windows (present in McGraw-Hill, too), a cantilevered tower mass, a clear expression in the structure of the difference between the vertical service core and the horizontal office areas. It is a handsome tower, with more dignity and subtlety than any pure International Style tower was to have until the Seagram Building. The Philadelphia Saving Fund Society building owed a considerable debt to the Knut Lonberg-Holm entry in the Chicago Tribune competition, a crisp study in sleek black and white surfaces—a reminder

The Philadelphia Saving Fund Society. Howe and Lescaze, 1932.

not only that the Tribune competition continued to be influential even in the 1930's, but that some of its most avant-garde entries had at long last begun to find a sympathetic reception among American architects and clients.

The powerful modernism of Philadelphia Saving Fund Society was hardly universal in the early thirties, of course, and the building was certainly controversial. The act of commissioning such a structure in conservative Philadelphia in 1929 must go down as one of the great leaps of architectural faith on the part of any major client in the twentieth century. "None like it had been built, and only rarely, as in the Chicago Tribune competition of 1922 and the projects for tall buildings by Mies and Le Corbusier, had anything near its size even been imagined in the vocabularies of either the first or second phase of the International Style," as Robert Stern has written. But there were a number of buildings of the time that, if not so advanced esthetically, nonetheless summed up certain other, less rigorous, concerns of the period. Perhaps foremost among these was the new Waldorf-Astoria Hotel on Park Avenue, of 1931, by Schultze and Weaver; its twin Art Deco towers and solid limestone masses looked back to the mid-twenties, to the great mountainous masses of Hugh Ferriss, but within was a dazzling array of ballrooms and shops and restaurants and nightclubs, more varied activity than any sin-

The Waldorf-Astoria Hotel, New York. Schultze and Weaver, 1931. The General Electric Building is visible uptown, and the Chrysler, Chanin, and Park Central buildings downtown.

97

Early model of Rockefeller Center showing an oval building in place of the present central promenade.

gle skyscraper had ever contained. Suddenly it seemed that the whole world—or at least the whole world of fantasy—could be contained within a single tower.

It could reasonably be said that everything the twenties and early thirties had been striving toward—a coherent yet romantic expression of the tower and a rational organization of the various urban functions within the skyscraper—came together in the mid-1930's in a vast project in the middle of Manhattan: Rockefeller Center. The Center was originally conceived in 1927 as a result of the Metropolitan Opera Company's need for a new home; John D. Rockefeller, Jr., was assisting the company in acquiring the land and developing the blocks around the planned opera house for commercial use to subsidize the company's operation. But the Depression, combined with political uncertainties within the opera company's management, led to the Metropolitan's withdrawal from the project; Rockefeller was left with the entire vast parcel, and he proceeded to develop it as what might be considered the nation's first large-scale, privately financed, mixed-use urban renewal project.

The architects were a consortium of three firms: Reinhard and Hofmeister; Corbett, Harrison, and MacMurray; and Hood and Fouilhoux. The plans, however, were based largely on early studies by Benjamin Wistar Morris, who had been the opera company's consulting architect; when the opera company withdrew, Reinhard and Hofmeister turned the Morris schemes into a straightforward plan calling for a tall central tower surrounded by lower buildings with an open plaza in the center. It was a formal, axial plan, symmetrical in its layout and rather Beaux-Arts in feeling, despite the skyscraper that had become the centerpiece.

But if Morris, who later resigned, and Reinhard and Hofmeister provided the basic scheme for Rockefeller Center, it was Raymond Hood, Harvey Wiley Corbett, and Wallace K. Harrison who carried the plan through. They made crucial changes, some a result of esthetic preferences, others a result of changing economic or programmatic needs as the vast development progressed. What emerged was a brilliant blend of Beaux-Arts and modern leanings, a set of towers and plazas and theaters

Raymond Hood, Wallace K. Harrison, and Andrew Reinhard gathered around the plaster model for La Maison Française and the British Empire Building.

The setbacks of the RCA Building, the centerpiece of Rockefeller Center.

and shops that seem at once to possess a strong, classicizing order and a sense of lively, almost spontaneous urban vitality.

The centerpiece, and the one skyscraper in the complex that can truly be called a masterwork, is the 70-story RCA Building. Its massing was largely the work of Hood, who took the simple slab Reinhard and Hofmeister had projected for the central location and sculpted it into an enormously graceful form. What Hood did was add a series of thin, cascading setbacks to each of the long sides of the slab as well as to its eastern front, setbacks that seemed almost to turn the building into a series of floating planes. It was a purely visual gesture—the slab, a dramatically new form (while it had been proposed by Wright as early as 1920, in his San Francisco Press Building, it had never actually been used for such a large office structure), did not require the setbacks to satisfy zoning ordinances, and indeed, as Alan Balfour has pointed out, Hood's use of them could almost have been considered retrogressive. The theorists of the International Style strongly disapproved of setbacks—they were a weakness in the McGraw-Hill Building to Hitchcock and Johnson, for example. But Hood's brilliant sense of composition was clearly again at work: he realized that a slab alone would have power but no real poetry to

it, and by cutting it back subtly its fundamental strength could not only be retained, but could be enhanced.

From the slender east front, the RCA Building appears almost too narrow to make sense at its great height. But here again the setbacks help, by offering a sense of depth and perspective that a purely abstract slab would not have. Equally important to this building's appearance—as to that of its neighbors—was the sheathing the architects devised, a skin of vertical strips of Indian limestone with dark metal recessed spandrels. The materials are different, but the effect of sleek verticality is similar to that of Hood and Howells's Daily News Building. Yet at Rockefeller Center there is also a sense of dignity that is missing at the Daily News; these buildings, for all their energy, seem solid and secure, designed for the ages in a way that Chrysler, for instance, does not.

Rockefeller Center's genius is that it exists at—indeed, it creates—a point of intersection between a number of things that would seem unable to coexist. It is strongly classicizing, yet it is lively and energetic; its layout is formal and axial, yet it is full of informal surprises; its conception was fundamentally commercial, yet it offered more to the public than many true civic structures. What is most significant from the standpoint of skyscraper design, however, is that it represented the first time skyscrapers had been conceived as a group. None of the Rockefeller Center buildings, not even the RCA Building, could exist alone; each needs the context created by the others to achieve its meaning. The skyscraper before Rockefeller Center had been conceived of as an isolated unit, as a tower standing alone; even buildings as well-integrated into their surroundings as the American Radiator, or buildings as varied in the functions they included as the Waldorf-Astoria, were independent structures, towers that did not need or demand connections to other buildings. Rockefeller Center changed that: it created a new model, a model of the skyscraper as part of a coherent composition of other skyscrapers. The arrangement had both esthetic and social implications, for it made possible not only the visual ordering of skyscraper cities, but the articulate organization of varied uses. The Center's accomplishment, in its way, was as significant as that of Woolworth and of the Wainwright Building before that—for after Rockefeller Center, the possibilities for the skyscraper would never again be the same.

"Atlas," by Lee Lawrie, stands in the forecourt of the International Building of Rockefeller Center.

"American Progress," the great mural in the lobby of the RCA Building, by José Maria Sert.

Opposite: Rockefeller Center, with the RCA Building in the center, New York. Rockefeller Center Associated Architects (Benjamin Wistar Morris; Reinhard & Hofmeister; Corbett, Harrison and MacMurray; Hood and Fouilhoux), 1932–40.

CHAPTER SEVEN

THE TRIUMPH OF MODERNISM

Rockefeller Center's main group of buildings was not completed until 1940, when John D. Rockefeller, Jr., personally drove the last rivet in the U.S. Rubber (now Simon and Schuster) Building. So not only did the complex dominate the decade of the thirties, it spanned it. And it effectively closed the period of prewar skyscrapers, for while there was a small amount of other construction in the late 1930's and early 1940's, nothing of real significance was built— the combined effects of the Depression and the war made tall business buildings unthinkable.

It was not until the end of the decade that construction of large-scale buildings began again in earnest, and by then, architects and builders faced a different world. The Chrysler Building, symbol of the jazz age, was 20 years old—older than the Woolworth Building had been when Chrysler itself was built. The daring Philadelphia Savings Fund Society building, symbol of all that was new and innovative, was 18 years old, nearly as venerable as Chrysler. The idea of great height was no longer startling—children born when the Empire State Building opened, in 1931, were themselves nearly adults. The city of great towers had become a commonplace, and there was little, it must have seemed, that architects and buildings could do to top their efforts of the past.

Architecture itself was at something of a crossroads after the war. The historicists' picturesque revivalism, the use of bits and pieces of Gothic and classical and Moorish styles, had lingered through the 1930's, its power weakening as its best practitioners retired, died, or, like George Howe, chose to give in to the developing modern movement. By 1950 revivalism had all but died out, and so had Art Deco, that spirited style of streamlined or Aztec-like ornament that had so dominated the late twenties and early thirties. Art Deco was far newer a style than revivalism, but perhaps it seemed too characteristic of the energy and spirit of the prewar years; a society christened by World War II could not give in so easily to Art Deco's naive romanticism.

Whatever the cause, the late forties and early fifties were a time for pragmatism. The economics of large-scale construction had changed too—there were no longer as many craftsmen available to do the elaborate handwork that ornamental styles, including Art Deco, required;

Opposite: The Seagram Building, New York. Mies van der Rohe and Philip Johnson, 1958.

103

The Look Building at 488 Madison Avenue, New York. Emery Roth and Sons, 1950.

Universal Pictures Building at 445 Park Avenue, New York. Kahn and Jacobs, 1947.

buildings were becoming more machine-made, more vulnerable to standardization, which in turn made architects more sympathetic to the preachings of the modern movement in its call for new materials, simple forms, and austere surfaces free of ornament.

It was after 1950, then, that modernism truly began to flourish in the United States—not for the noble rationalism its original proponents back in the twenties and thirties believed it had, but as an economic necessity. Modern buildings were cheaper and more practical to erect—this was true whether the building was a six-room house or a 60-story skyscraper.

The skyscrapers of the early 1950's were, for the most part, an undistinguished lot. The majority were built in a style that has never been named, and has been overlooked by most historians; it is something of a hybrid between the old-fashioned masonry setback buildings of the prewar era and the sleeker buildings of the International Style. The better buildings of this style, structures like the Look Building of 1950, at 488 Madison Avenue in New York, by Emery Roth and Sons, and the Universal Pictures Building of 1947, at 445 Park Avenue in New York, by

Kahn and Jacobs, do sit handsomely, if not lightly, on the street, how-ever, and they manage to be compatible with both older and newer neighbors. The essence of the style is an exterior wall of limestone (in 445 Park) or brick (in 488 Madison, and most of the others) set in hori-zontal bands, which alternate with horizontal bands of windows. The massing is determined largely by zoning: it takes the building out to the property line for the first 12 stories, then sets back neatly several times for roughly 10 stories more. The whole is a bit squat, but not awkward.

The effect is not unlike a wedding cake, but the large mass at the base holds the street line well. The use of masonry is significant, for it gives the buildings a necessary visual weight and ties them to the older buildings that, for a while at least, surrounded them, and it offsets the stark effect of the strip windows. At best, however, these were still dull, squat buildings moving cautiously into a new time; it is no surprise that the most interesting aspect of the Look Building is not its overall style but its rounded corners—a detail which seems clearly to derive from the Starrett-Lehigh Building (page 126), the great 1931 factory-warehouse on the Manhattan waterfront.

The real innovation at the beginning of the fifties came not in a com-mercial skyscraper but in an institutional one: the United Nations Sec-retariat Building in New York, a 39-story tower whose form was a pure slab unmodulated by setbacks and unadorned by any decoration. The UN tower was the work of an international board of architects under the chairmanship of Wallace K. Harrison, but the essential idea derived from a sketch by Le Corbusier. The narrow slab was set so that its long walls, which were of green glass, faced east and west, and its short walls, which were of white marble, faced north and south.

The United Nations tower was a stunning abstraction—a pure sculpture, really, woefully impractical in its orientation (complete walls of glass facing west and east play havoc with the air-conditioning bill) and not much more sensible in its solid end walls, which denied win-dows to a significant number of offices. Moreover, as Lewis Mumford has pointed out, the decision to make the dominant architectural ele-ment of the United Nations grouping the Secretariat, rather than the

The United Nations, New York. International Committee under Wallace K. Harrison, 1950.

The United Nations from across the East River in Brooklyn.

105

Lever House, New York. Skidmore, Owings, and Merrill, 1952.

The plaza of Lever House.

General Assembly, was an odd symbolic choice—it seemed to stand for the triumph of the bureaucracy over other aspects of the organization.

Still, the Secretariat did bring to New York its first glass curtain wall, and this alone made it seem like a bold emblem of progress—the idea of a tower that would appear to be sheathed only in glass had been around since Mies van der Rohe's schemes of the 1920's but had never been realized. The fact that the Secretariat stood alone, or nearly alone, on an open site made it more special still—a symbol of an age that saw itself as free, unbound by the constraints of the past, either esthetic or technological.

In 1952, just after the Secretariat's completion, Skidmore, Owings, and Merrill, the architectural firm that more than any other was to influence American skyscraper design in the next two decades, constructed its first major skyscraper. The building was Lever House, on Park Avenue in New York, and the designer was Skidmore partner Gordon Bunshaft; the structure was to be the headquarters of Lever Brothers, the soap company. It was commissioned by Charles Luckman, an architect who had become Lever Brothers' president and who later began a lucrative, though hardly distinguished, architectural practice of his own. Indeed, it is no exaggeration to say that Luckman's greatest contribution to architecture was making Lever House possible, for this building was to have as widespread an influence as any skyscraper of the early 1950's. Lever changed the prevailing notions of what a skyscraper could be—it went beyond even the United Nations in making pure abstraction a virtue, and it celebrated light and openness in a way that must have seemed stunning to a city accustomed to blocks and blocks of limestone and granite.

What Bunshaft did was scoop out a block of Park Avenue and insert two slabs of stainless steel and glass, one set horizontally on columns over an open first floor, the other poised vertically above. Suddenly the tight city was opened up, both at ground level and above: light poured in, open space flowed around. It was a splendid act of corporate philanthropy, too: the tower was smaller than the maximum that zoning laws would have permitted—so much smaller, in fact, that in the 1970's, as development pressures bore down sharply on Park Avenue, the Lever Brothers company was forced to turn away several offers from builders eager to tear Lever House down and replace it with a skyscraper two or three times its size.

Lever's abstract beauty remains powerful, more than a quarter century after its completion, and its genuine modesty of scale brings to the streetscape a sense of humanism that has been desperately lacking in many more recent glass towers. Still, the building seems flawed by today's standards—the break with the street wall of Park Avenue, so liberating in the 1950's, now seems needless and not a little narcissistic. The open ground floor, which seemed the very embodiment of enlightened urbanism when it was new, seems now somewhat dull and sterile, its public space little used. And the premise of "structural honesty" on which the building was said to be based is, of course, an exaggeration. The double-slab form is a pure composition, as much as was the crown of the Chrysler Building; and the use of spandrel glass—the glass that covers the structure between the floors, making the entire outside look as if it were made of glass—is not structural honesty at all, but merely a modernist brand of ornament.

Less ambitious, in its way, but less compromised by the passage of time, is the early masterwork of Skidmore, Owings, and Merrill's Chicago office, the Inland Steel Building of 1957, on West Monroe Street. Here the notion was an expression of the differences in function between the sections of each floor that housed offices and those that housed elevators, stairs, and other service elements; what resulted was a glass box with a metal box standing beside it. Again, as in Lever, there was arbitrary abstraction, but there is also an exceedingly elegant bearing to this structure—Inland Steel may not require its metal-enclosed service core, but the core does bring a considerable panache to the overall form.

Oddly, the differences between Lever House and Inland Steel seemed to parallel the differences in approach that had divided New York and Chicago for generations—the coming of modernism had not entirely changed the two cities' basically opposing attitudes. Lever House, for all its modernist credentials, still seems somewhat theatrical in comparison with Inland Steel; its abstractions are more those of pure

The Inland Steel Building, Chicago. Skidmore, Owings, and Merrill, 1957.

Mies van der Rohe.

visual pleasure, of pure composition, while Inland Steel's abstractions are based more directly on an expression of use and structure.

Indeed, Chicago in the 1950's was beginning to acquire some of the characteristics of Chicago in the 1880's. Mies van der Rohe, who settled in the city after fleeing the Nazis in the late 1930's, had attracted around him a number of architects who leaned toward the International Style— among them, in fact, the early partners of Skidmore, Owings, and Merrill. Mies set a tone of moral authority and intellectual rigor that was to permeate Chicago architecture through the 1960's and 1970's; there was a sense, whether in his own practice at the Skidmore office or elsewhere, that the austere glass-and-steel boxes of the International Style were the only really appropriate architectural path to follow in the postwar years. And Mies's presence assured that the tenets of the style—its great attention to proportion, to scale, to materials, and to details—were generally adhered to.

Mies himself was more than a teacher; he was an active architect in Chicago, and his career as a skyscraper builder had begun in the late 1940's, with the Promontory Apartments, an early-postwar high-rise on

Lake Shore Drive Apartments, Chicago. Mies van der Rohe, 1952.

the city's Southside. More significant were the Lake Shore Drive Apartments of 1952, a pair of towers at 860–880 Lake Shore Drive that were the first apartment buildings anywhere in the country to be sheathed entirely in glass. The buildings were slender, elegantly proportioned towers sitting on columns, with glass-enclosed lobbies; as much even as the UN tower, these, too, seemed able to suggest a new time—a world in which not only offices but also homes could float in the air, enclosed merely by glass.

Glass was surely the material of the decade. Relatively inexpensive, it could be used to sheathe almost any kind of building form, from the elegant abstraction of Lever House to New York buildings such as 400 and 410 Park Avenue, undistinguished towers by Emery Roth and Sons—put up in 1957 and 1959—that were identical to the masonry buildings with horizontal window strips of the early part of the decade except for their glass coatings. The notion that glass buildings could be difficult to heat and cool seemed unimportant in an age of inexpensive energy; the relative anonymity of the "glass box" seemed of little concern to anyone except architectural critics, and even they were frequently swayed by the romance of the new. As the fifties wore on, the downtown of many American cities, and not merely New York and Chicago, began to acquire glass boxes that might, in some distant way, be said to have related to the work of Mies van der Rohe. It was surely their inspiration, but the actual buildings bore no more real a connection to Mies's designs than a Ford does to a Rolls-Royce. Even those few towers that were not sheathed in glass, such as Carson and Lundin's Tishman Building of 1957 at 666 Fifth Avenue, or Harrison and Abramovitz's Alcoa Building of 1955 in Pittsburgh, both of which were covered in a decorative aluminum sheathing, remained boxes, with flat tops and a prefabricated feel to them. (The joke going around New York in the late 1950's was that the Tishman Building was the box that Lever House came in.)

The notion of the skyscraper as a romantic object, as a building that might have some degree of symbolic quality to it, seemed to disappear. Most of the architects of the time eschewed any overt symbolism for their buildings, although in spite of this their structures still managed to convey a certain kind of message—a message of a rather faceless corporate bureaucracy housed in boxes that looked like other boxes. In this sense, then, the skyscrapers of the 1950's were apt. If nothing else, they did give architectural expression to the changing nature of the American corporate structure that caused them to be built.

There was one notable exception to the trend, a building so small—it was 15 stories high—that it barely seemed a skyscraper by the standards of the day. It was the Price Tower, in Bartlesville, Oklahoma, completed in 1955 to the designs of Frank Lloyd Wright, who had been trying to get a skyscraper built since just after the turn of the century. The Price Tower, built as the headquarters for a local company, contained apartments as well; it was based upon a brilliant scheme by Wright for an apartment tower planned by the New York church St. Mark's in the Bowerie in 1928. The Depression killed the project then, but Wright resurrected it in the early 1950's. The tower is full of Wright's tense, energetic desire to break out of the box—it is a study in angles and cantilevers, tensile and taut, a building with far more ideas than its modest size seems to justify. Had it been built at its original 20-story height in 1928, it would have been a major building of the twen-

The Alcoa Building, Pittsburgh. Harrison and Abramovitz, 1955.

tieth century; in 1955, in reduced form, it seemed more a curiosity, a model to echo an idea.

There were a few more conventional exceptions to the general level of banality that characterized much of the second half of the decade. Skidmore, Owings, and Merrill's headquarters for Pepsi-Cola (now the Olivetti Building) at 500 Park Avenue in New York, completed at the decade's end, is an elegant box of glass and aluminum, floating on piers but respectful of the street and of the scale of its neighbors—a jewel of metal and glass that plays off well against the older masonry buildings that surround it.

But the high point of the fifties was unquestionably the completion in 1958 in New York of the Seagram Building, Mies van der Rohe's first major corporate skyscraper. It was designed in association with Philip Johnson, and it came about in an odd way: Phyllis Lambert, the architect daughter of Samuel Bronfman, head of Joseph E. Seagram and Sons, was so distressed when she learned that her father had retained Charles Luckman to design the building that she flew back from Paris to persuade him to hire an architect of international reputation. Father indulged daughter, putting her in charge of a search committee; she later

Price Tower, Bartlesville, Oklahoma. Frank Lloyd Wright, 1955.

Opposite: The Pepsi-Cola Building (now the Olivetti Building), New York. Skidmore, Owings, and Merrill, 1960.

110

The Seagram Building at night, with the Waldorf-Astoria in the background.

wrote that she had considered Frank Lloyd Wright for the job, but felt that his work represented the frontier mentality of an America then gone, and that Le Corbusier's forms would not be a "good influence" in New York. Mies was the architect of the day, she thought; "Mies forces you in. You have to go deeper. You might think this austere strength, this ugly beauty, is terribly severe. It is, and yet all the more beauty in it."

Seagram is a 38-story tower of bronze and glass, set back from Park Avenue on a deep plaza, with green Italian marble rails as benches along its sides and two great fountains in its foreground. The tower rises sheer, without setbacks. There is a 2-story lobby of travertine, glass-enclosed like the bases of Mies's apartment buildings; ordinary store-fronts are banned, and those commercial uses that do exist—the stunning Four Seasons restaurant and its companion, the Brasserie—are tucked discreetly into the rear.

Seagram is as refined a glass tower as has ever been built, a temple to reason—a tower built to elucidate the Miesian principles of order, logic, and clarity in all things. It is not quite what it would seem, however—

112

Mies van der Rohe was far more interested in having his buildings appear to be structurally simple than actually to have them be structurally simple. Louis Kahn, for example, was fond of calling Seagram "a beautiful lady in hidden corsets," because the "pure" Miesian skin hides a number of other supports. And the I-beams running down the façade and marble-paneled false windows on the side are somewhat mannered and ornamental, not the true outgrowth of technology that Mies liked to suggest his buildings were.

No matter. If the myths that have surrounded this building (and the rest of Mies's work) do not entirely reflect reality, this does not diminish Seagram's standing as one of the great buildings of the twentieth century. The bronze curtain wall is serene, the proportions are exquisite, and the detailing is as perfect as that of any postwar skyscraper anywhere. Even the lavatory fixtures and lettering on the lobby mailboxes were specially designed.

Seagram, like Rockefeller Center, was a certain kind of model—it revealed a new set of possibilities for skyscrapers. In this case, unfortunately, the implications were less benign—for while a Rockefeller Center done in less capable hands would still offer a variety of activities for public use, an imitation Seagram would be only a banal tower, a box little different from what had preceded it. This is exactly what was to happen in the years to follow as New York's city planners, entranced by the beauty of Seagram's sheer rise from a wide, open plaza, changed the city's zoning laws to encourage more towers massed as Seagram had been. The results proved Seagram, although a great work of art, a poor model.

The Seagram plaza.

CHAPTER EIGHT

THE BATTLE WON—
ABSTRACTION AND PUBLIC SPACE

There has been a tendency in the architecture of twentieth-century New York to present an idea first in its best form and then to compromise it, rather than refine it in later versions. So it was, unfortunately, with Rockefeller Center, which has never even been approached in quality by the multiskyscraper groupings that followed it, elsewhere as well as in its own city, and so it has been, too, with the Seagram Building. The decade following Seagram's completion was the era of the sheer tower, the skyscraper soaring straight up from an open plaza, and not one of Seagram's followers equaled the excellence of the original. Some of the imitators, like the tawdry group of skyscrapers on Manhattan's Third Avenue, were merely cheap and confused; others, like Mies van der Rohe's own Federal Center grouping in Chicago of 1969, were refined and elegant but lacked the extraordinary attention to detail—not to mention the sense of energetic, stunning freshness—that had marked Seagram.

Eero Saarinen was an architect whose formal inventiveness, although not always subtle, had very much affected the 1950's, and it is no surprise that his single attempt at a skyscraper, the CBS Building in New York, was one of the most talked-about buildings of the 1960's. Completed in 1965, after Saarinen's death, CBS follows the preference of the time in its massing—it is a boxy tower, rising straight for 38 floors without a single setback—but it breaks sharply from the prevailing style in its form. The tower is clad in triangular columns of dark gray granite, behind which are set gray granite spandrels; the overall effect of the façade is of a grid, with a slight emphasis on the vertical.

The building has great dignity to it—it would be hard for anything with so much charcoal gray granite not to have—but it stands almost maddeningly aloof from its surroundings. CBS exacerbates a tendency that began with those 1950's masterpieces Lever House and Seagram to reject any direct connection to, or even any overt acknowledgment of, the architectural context of which it is a part. CBS stands back from the sidewalk on all sides; its plaza is even set a few steps below street level to emphasize the disconnection. The building faces the Avenue of the Americas, a major thoroughfare, yet there is no door between any of the somber granite columns on that side—too close a tie, perhaps, to the

Rockefeller Center Extension. Part of the original plan for Rockefeller Center, these towers along the west side of the Avenue of the Americas, all by Harrison, Abramowitz, and Harris, did not go up until much later. They are the Exxon (1973), McGraw-Hill (1973), and Celanese (1974) buildings.

Opposite: The CBS Building, New York. Eero Saarinen, 1965.

115

Worcester County National Bank, Worcester, Massachusetts. Roche and Dinkeloo, 1974.

Knights of Columbus Tower, New Haven. Roche and Dinkeloo, 1967.

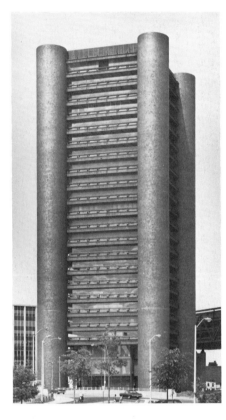

chaotic architecture of the rest of the street, from which Saarinen seems to have gone to pains to dissociate his structure. But most telling is the building's purely abstract form—the box is varied in no way at all to take into account the life of the city around it.

Saarinen's firm—and to some extent his direction—was taken over by Kevin Roche and John Dinkeloo, who had been among his senior associates; they made their first mark in skyscraper design with a relatively small but visually powerful building, the Knights of Columbus headquarters in New Haven. Here, four massive cylinders form the corners, and the floors are supported by great Cor-ten rusted steel beams, which span the distance between the columns like great bridges. It is all a rather elaborate piece of showmanship. The towers are somewhat too heavy to be in proportion to the distance between them, and they do not contain elevators or other service elements, as they might logically appear to do; these functions are clustered in a hidden central service core.

The Knights of Columbus tower calls to mind the ambitious early 1960's megastructure schemes of the English Archigram group and the Japanese metabolist school: it was a symbolic vision of a brave and technologically awesome new world, a world of immense structures that ap-

116

peared more to set themselves into the landscape than to grow from it. The design was far too ambitious for the modest size of the tower—it is only 23 stories high—and this building shares the weakness common to so many of its contemporaries, the need to stand alone, a thing apart from the urban environment within which it sits. It is a tendency Kevin Roche, the firm's chief designer, did not pursue as zealously in his later skyscrapers; while buildings such as the Worcester (County) National Bank, of 1974, in Worcester, Massachusetts, were clearly sculptural, they often make gestures to accommodate themselves to their context.

Indeed, Roche's United Nations Plaza hotel and office complex of 1976, in New York City, is almost an example of the extent to which abstractions can be made to relate to the city around it. Although the skin of blue-green reflective glass is arranged in a gridiron of panes that obscures any sense of inner structure, its color relates well to that of the

Model showing the complete hotel and office building at United Nations Plaza.

First phase of United Nations Plaza, New York. Roche and Dinkeloo, 1976.

Secretariat Building across the street. And the shape, which seems rather arbitrary at first glance—there is a nipped-in corner at the southeast and some 45-degree setbacks on the north—in fact plays off quite subtly against the Secretariat's even slab.

This is one of the most beautiful towers of the postwar period, despite the fact that it breaks virtually every common-sense rule of highrise construction. The exquisite skin covers the structure like a blanket, permitting no expression of the changing uses that characterize the building (it contains offices on its lower floors, hotel rooms above) or of its floor divisions. It is all pure abstraction, made gentle and urbane by Roche's skill.

I. M. Pei and his chief design partner, Henry Cobb, have been through a similar evolution during these two decades. The Pei office produced a number of handsome towers of reinforced concrete throughout the 1960's and early 1970's, buildings such as Kips Bay Plaza (1965) and University Towers (now Silver Towers) Housing (1960–65) in New York, or the Society Hill Tower Project (1962) in Philadelphia, all of which have rhythmic façades of wafflelike concrete grids. But Pei turned to glass for his most significant later skyscraper, the John Hancock Tower at Copley Square in Boston, which he designed with Cobb. This tower ini-

University Towers Housing, New York. I. M. Pei, 1960–65.

Kips Bay Plaza, New York. I. M. Pei, 1965.

118

tially became famous for reasons other than its esthetics, when, in 1972, just before completion, its windows began to fall out. Eventually they all had to be replaced, delaying the building's opening for several years and producing one of the most complex webs of architectural malpractice suits in American history. For at least a year, the original windows were removed and replaced with wooden panels, which became such a fixture on the Boston skyline that the leading joke around the city was that the structure should be renamed the U.S. Plywood Building.

When it was finally opened, with new and different windows, in 1975, the building turned out to be something of an esthetic triumph. As Roche had done at the United Nations Plaza, Cobb created here an abstraction in glass that by its shape took into account the lines and forces of the surrounding buildings and open spaces. The John Hancock Tower is a parallelogram, quite slender, with a short base to carry across neighboring cornices and a nip in the glass façade running all the way up the 60-story height to provide some sense of texture.

It is a stunning object, and it is not surprising that Bostonians, who mocked the building rather mercilessly during its glass crisis, came generally to admire it. But the pure abstraction of the Hancock Tower, for all the accommodations it attempts to make to its surroundings, does remain rather at odds with its context. The building shares Copley Square with two of the greatest nineteenth-century public buildings in the United States—Henry Hobson Richardson's Trinity Church and

The base of the John Hancock Tower, with Trinity Church (Henry Hobson Richardson, 1877) reflected on its front and the Copley Plaza Hotel (Henry Hardenbergh, 1912) along its side. Below: John Hancock Tower, Boston. I.M. Pei and Henry Cobb, 1975.

119

Prudential Center, Boston. Charles Luckman, 1963.

Peachtree Center and the Hyatt Regency Hotel, Atlanta. John Portman, 1967 on.

McKim, Mead, and White's Boston Public Library—and they, along with Henry Hardenbergh's Copley Plaza Hotel, establish a tone that Hancock clearly violates, if only by its great height. But it is the tower's material that seems most jarring: Glass is thin, brittle, tense, whereas the masonry of the earlier buildings is deep, solid, self-assured. The older buildings are rich, mysterious works, full of a sense of human frailty; the glass tower is a technological object, depending for its value not on a sense of the presence of human effort but on a sense of its absence.

There are further problems with the esthetic of a building like Hancock, problems that by no means afflict this building the most seriously. The use of reflective glass, a material that has gained greater and greater popularity (not the least of its attractions is its ability to reduce the high cost of air-conditioning the great towers), tends to heighten any degree of abstraction that the building's overall shape has given it. In the case of Hancock, the extreme reflectivity meant that the building literally mirrored Trinity Church, which rendered Hancock even less "real" an object in terms of conventional perception; it seemed not like a building at all but like a great slender mirror stood up against the sky.

And even if the premise that the skyscraper is fundamentally an abstract object is accepted—forgetting how far this takes us from the humanism of the early skyscraper designers—this in turn invites an equally troubling problem. There is no logical way to insert into an abstract object a door, to give it a canopy, or to install upon it any kind of sign without fundamentally violating its abstraction. At Hancock Cobb used a series of glass bubbles, projecting out from the glass façade, as entrance canopies; they look both silly in themselves and inappropriate to the esthetic of the building, as if the architect had been desperate to add a humanizing element and had picked one that seemed to come from the circus. Probably Kevin Roche had the best solution: at the United Nations Plaza building he peeled off a portion of the glass skin toward the bottom, turning it into a canopy without violating the integrity of the overall form.

The movement toward the making of abstract shapes was one of two trends that marked the time; the other was a recognition, long overdue, that the urbanistic values embodied in Rockefeller Center were in fact urgent ones, and the subsequent striving to give new skyscrapers some of the same sense of civic use. It became more common to include retail space in skyscraper complexes, and public plazas began to be seen as desirable in themselves, not merely as devices to set off the form of a tower.

Many of the early complexes were distinguished neither architecturally nor urbanistically. Boston's Prudential Center, completed in 1963, by Charles Luckman, is a collection of mediocre towers arranged around an austere and ugly mall, the esthetic of a suburban shopping center thrust into an unwilling downtown. It was a crude violation of the spirit of Rockefeller Center, as was its contemporary, Hartford's Constitution Plaza, which committed the added sin of being set on a platform to remove it entirely from the ongoing life of the city around it. Somewhat better urbanistically, if not architecturally, were two complexes initiated in the late 1960's by the architect and developer John Portman: Peachtree Center in Atlanta and Embarcadero Center in San Francisco. Portman had studied both Rockefeller Center and the Tivoli Gardens in Copenhagen, and the results show. His complexes are marked by considerable attention to social interaction through the provision of cafés,

120

Embarcadero Center, San Francisco.
John Portman, 1971.

Parklike alcove in the Embarcadero.

parklike alcoves, and ample retail space. For the Peachtree Center's widely imitated Hyatt Regency Hotel, Portman devised an immense atrium, making the hotel in effect an indoor plaza and a piece of theater second to none in American urban architecture of its time. Portman's esthetic, however, was somewhat at odds with his humanistic bent: he leaned toward massive structures of exposed concrete and glass, bold assemblages of simple geometric forms, which were often not so far from the abstractions of other contemporary architects. For his Peachtree Plaza, Detroit Plaza, and Los Angeles Bonaventure hotels, he used tall glass cylinders, standing alone in Atlanta and Detroit, and bunched together in a group of five in Los Angeles.

Thus, Portman's great concern for human activity was not really expressed through respect for the traditional city—his urbanism was all indoors, not out. In many ways Portman was providing an alternative to existing downtowns as much as an enhancement of them, because the immense geometric forms, the huge glass cylinders or the atriums filled with cocktail lounges ("like going through Piranesi with a martini in your hand," architect Charles Moore once said of a Portman space) were not only fundamentally abstract themselves, but they were much bigger in scale than most conventional buildings. The Detroit hotel and the second Atlanta hotel were each 70 stories high, with lakes in the lobby and revolving cocktail lounges on top. It was increasingly easy to think of even the best of Portman's multibuilding complexes as being designed only for inhabitants of a fast-moving, flashy world, a world of airports and expense accounts, not for the citizens who lived in these cities and used the neighboring buildings every day. So, too, with Welton Becket's Hyatt Regency Reunion of 1978 in Dallas, the best of the many Portman imitations erected around the country in the wake of the Atlanta Hotel's success. This one has not only an atrium within but reflecting glass without, and it mounts up in setbacks, managing to unite the traditions of both mirrored abstraction and interior urbanism. The Hyatt Regency

Hyatt Regency Reunion, Dallas.
Welton Becket, 1978.

The IDS Center, Minneapolis. Johnson and Burgee, 1972.

Reunion gleams at the edge of a freeway, beckoning like the Emerald City.

Surprisingly, it was Philip Johnson who, in 1972, brought the various streams of the period together in a building that was to become a model for the humanistic skyscraper, as Rockefeller Center had been before. The building was the IDS Center in Minneapolis, headquarters for the large financial services firm. Due largely to the urgings of Johnson's partner, John Burgee, the program was expanded from a simple office tower to include a hotel and a retail complex. Johnson, whose skyscraper experience at that time was limited to his work with Mies van der Rohe on the Seagram Building, the small but elegantly classicizing Kline Biology Tower of 1963 at Yale, and a number of unbuilt designs, produced a scheme by which a 51-story glass tower, a 19-story hotel, and a lower retail wing were all arranged around a central glass-covered court.

The tower's shape is roughly that of a flattened octagon, with its far diagonal sides cut into facets, creating a zigzag effect. The faceting seems to break up the large mass, reducing its visual impact, as well as bringing variety to the form; since it also added thirty-two corner offices per floor, it could be said to have had a practical purpose, and not

123

Lehman Brothers Headquarters design, New York. Johnson and Burgee.

Logan Circle Project, Philadelphia. Johnson and Burgee.

to have been solely a formal gesture. The tower is sheathed in a lightly reflecting pale-blue glass; mounting up like a pile of glass bricks are the transparent roof sections of the court, which is like a great crystal tent pitched in the middle of the city. The complex is surrounded by shops on its outside, to enhance the sense of connection with the city; it is Minneapolis's largest structure by far, yet it appears, like Rockefeller Center, to be a modest and benign presence more than an imposing one.

IDS was Johnson and Burgee's first built skyscraper, but it followed a number of unrealized projects worthy of our attention, if only because they prefigure directions a number of architects were soon to follow. For Lehman Brothers in lower Manhattan the firm designed a tower with V-shaped indentations in each corner and an 8-story galleria passing through the base. For Logan Circle in Philadelphia, Johnson and Burgee designed a pair of towers around a central plaza; the massing, a curious cross between 1930's setback design and 1960's diagonals, looks remarkably like the nip-and-tuck towers that architects desperate to break out of the box were to devise in such quantity in the early 1980's. But here it makes good urban sense, for the shape relates clearly to the axes of Logan Circle.

Johnson and Burgee were to go on to do a number of the better skyscrapers of the 1970's, although their other successes tended to be more along the lines of abstraction. Rarely did they equal IDS's brilliant combination of formal beauty and urbanistic appropriateness. But Pennzoil Place, in Houston, completed in 1976, became the best-known building in that booming city's downtown with good reason: it was a pair of trapezoid-shaped towers, each sliced off at a 45-degree angle at the top, and joined at the bottom by a communal greenhouse lobby. This was pure abstraction, but it was dazzling—a city had not seen so recognizable a skyscraper top since the Empire State Building's. And the twin trapezoids, for all their energy, had a certain dignity, too—it was Johnson's gift that

Opposite: Pennzoil Place, Houston. Johnson and Burgee, 1976.

124

he was able to create an eye-catching form just right for the image of this city, a place eager to make its mark yet desirous of appearing strong and stable at the same time.

Johnson and Burgee also designed a remarkable pair of smaller towers for Houston called Post Oak Central. They were given identical skins based on the strip windows and curved corners of the Starrett-Lehigh Building in New York of 1931, an industrial landmark that somewhat prefigured the strip-window office buildings of the early 1950's. Johnson and Burgee exploited the nostalgic quality of the association to Starrett-Lehigh, making the glass and gray-metal panel façade look as streamlined as they could, alluding to the romance of Art Deco.

Johnson was to delve much deeper into historical allusion in his later skyscraper designs. But in his rebellion against the pure forms of Mies van der Rohe and in his move toward what might be called a more theatrical kind of skyscraper, he joined a number of less distinguished architects. Minoru Yamasaki, for one, had been covering towers with delicate tracery, an allusion to Gothic architecture, for some time: in some of his skyscrapers, like the IBM Building in Seattle of 1964, this practice came off as little more than precious and dull, but in others, such as the World Trade Center, the 110-story twin towers in lower Manhattan, finished

Starrett-Lehigh Building, New York. Russell and Walter Cory, with Yasuo Mitsui, 1931. Drawing by Richard Haas.

Post Oak Central, Houston. Johnson and Burgee, 1976 and 1978.

126

The plaza of the World Trade Center.

World Trade Center, New York.
Minoru Yamasaki, and Emery Roth and
Sons, 1976.

in 1976, it was almost sinister—the attempt to sheathe these large towers with a delicate coating was so obviously false that the entire project seems disingenuous.

The Trade Center's architecture was firmly rearguard—two identical towers, simply boxes, on a vast plaza. All retail functions were banished underground, and what was left was an austere street level reminiscent of the worst efforts of the 1960's urban renewal projects. The towers themselves took over the title of Manhattan's tallest buildings, but offered little except pure height to the skyline; their flat tops and huge masses had a deadening effect on the vista, altogether different from the lively slices into the sky of Chrysler and the Empire State. One should be grateful, however, that there were two towers and not just one—the two boxes do play off against each other rather successfully as minimalist sculpture; if one tower had existed alone the result would have been horrifyingly banal.

For all the dullness of the Trade Center's architecture, it did represent a number of technological innovations. First and foremost was the skin, which was not a "curtain wall" hung from a supporting frame, but a metal mesh that in fact supported a substantial share of the building's weight. It was a striking irony: the most advanced skyscraper in the world returning, in a sense, to a kind of load-bearing wall, to a version of exactly what the early makers of skyscrapers had given up. The Trade Center also contained the first new elevator system to be invented since

Building the World Trade Center.

Lower Manhattan from the Hudson River.

128

the double-deck car was first tried in the early 1930's—there are huge express cars that take all passengers to so-called sky lobbies at various intervals up the tower, where they are switched to local cars. Thus only a handful of upper-floor elevators need extend all the way through the building, robbing lower floors of valuable space.

Minoru Yamasaki's entrancement with technology and his fondness for romanticized forms are given full expression in the Rainier National Bank tower of 1978 in Seattle. This building was perhaps the culmination of the architect's attempts to explore curvilinear form: it is a box that is balanced on a concrete base that narrows toward the bottom, making the entire building appear to be poised on a tiny point, like a ballet dancer. It is visually startling, yet unlike Pennzoil, it creates a certain tension—the surprise of the initial form—that never resolves itself; the building seems always about to fall and is always a disturbing presence. It is something of an engineering trick, pure structural exhibitionism—

129

Transamerica Building, San Francisco. William Pereira, 1976.

Marina City, Chicago. Bertrand Goldberg, 1964.

at the expense of a certain kind of conventional appearance that seems an essential precondition of esthetic comfort.

No more conventional was William Pereira's Transamerica Building of 1976, in San Francisco. A pyramidal tower based on Pereira's never-built scheme of the 1960's for the American Broadcasting Company in New York, this structure rises to a sharp, narrow point. When it first went up, it was more controversial than any tower in the city's history, and with good reason: it is a jarring presence in that gentle city, and its details are crude. But Transamerica has turned out to be less destructive to San Francisco than many other, less unusual skyscrapers: its thin and eccentric shape in fact intrudes only slightly on the city's skyline. It is also one of the best examples of the skyscraper as image maker since Woolworth—the Transamerica Corporation uses the building as a symbol in its advertising and has made of it an internationally known icon.

The contorted shapes with which a number of architects were preoccupied seem not to have reached Chicago, where Mies still reigned supreme. Only one architect, Bertrand Goldberg, made a major mark by doing a different sort of work; his most important skyscraper was the Marina City complex in downtown Chicago, a pair of round concrete towers often likened to corncobs. Mies himself was active in the city, with the Federal Center of 1964–69 and the IBM Building of 1971, completed after his death, his most distinguished works. But Skidmore, Owings, and Merrill—such ardent followers of the master that they were once termed "three blind Mies"—were more active still. In association with C. F. Murphy and its outstanding designer, Jacques Brownson, Skidmore in 1965 completed the handsome Richard Daley Center,

Richard Daley Center, Chicago.
Skidmore, Owings, and Merrill, and
C. F. Murphy, 1965.

The Federal Center. Mies van der
Rohe, Chicago, 1964–69.

131

John Hancock Center, Chicago.
Skidmore, Owings, and Merrill, 1969.

which changed the conventional Miesian style into something tougher, harsher, less delicate, and, curiously, more similar in its proportions to the old Chicago window of before the turn of the century. But the firm's major accomplishments in Chicago were the city's two tallest buildings, the 95-story John Hancock Center of 1969, and the 110-story Sears Tower of 1974, which at 1,454 feet was the tallest building in the world.

John Hancock was a tall shaft that narrowed on all four sides as it moved toward the top. It proudly, almost arrogantly, displayed its structural reinforcements—huge X-braces cutting across the façade. It was a building of swagger, of enormous strength, although its shape made it a less than compatible neighbor on North Michigan Avenue. The tower seemed like a looming giant, a great cowboy stalking the town. Skidmore's attempt to make the form gentler by sheathing the bottom in travertine did little to help; in truth, it only added an uncomfortable, awkward tone to the structure.

Sears was no better at ground level—once again, there was an uneasy travertine sheathing, as if to hide the fact that these architects did not know how to make their skyscraper join the ground. It is far better in the sky. The building's structure is unusual—it is in effect a set of square tubes, virtually separate towers, bridled together. The tubes stop at different heights, giving the building a varied, stepped-down profile. It is a splendid allusion to the elaborate tops of old, but it emerges directly and logically out of structural expression. So at Sears, architects found a way in which the modernist idiom could be used for the creation of a romantic and rather nonmodernist result, the ornate top.

Chicago produced one other significant skyscraper in what might be called the late Miesian era. It was the 70-story Lake Point Tower of 1968 by Schipporeit and Heinrich. Although it was based on Mies's unbuilt plans from the 1920's for a glass tower of curving walls, there were significant differences from Mies's model. The tower was dark, and more of a conventional skyscraper than Mies's cantilevered structure would

Opposite: Sears Tower, Chicago.
Skidmore, Owings, and Merrill, 1974.

132

Lake Point Tower, Chicago.
Schipporeit and Heinrich, 1968.

have been; it was also set on a heavy, boxy base rather than directly on the ground. But it was a stunning, shimmering presence on the lakefront, its undulating façade expressing a lyricism that most latter-day Miesian buildings lacked.

The theatrics of Lake Point Tower might more appropriately have been part of New York's skyscraper tradition than Chicago's, though New York is not a city in which real estate developers are inclined to invest as much in housing as did the builders of Lake Point Tower. New York's tradition in privately built housing is simply too tightfisted. Ironically, it is only in the area of publicly assisted housing that any architectural quality is evident. Towers such as the red-brick Waterside Plaza of 1974, by Davis, Brody, and Associates, which has chamfered corners and is built out rather than set back at the top, were far more notable than most privately erected housing.

An erratic group of skyscrapers were built in New York during this period. They ranged from flamboyant attempts to exploit the city's theatrical tendencies to one building that seems better than anything else to

Opposite: Waterside Plaza, New York.
Davis, Brody, and Associates, 1974.

135

9 West 57th Street, New York. Skidmore, Owings, and Merrill, 1974. Drawing by Richard Haas.

summarize all that was best about the 1960's and 1970's. The flamboyant buildings, from Skidmore, Owings, and Merrill's New York office in 1974, were a pair of towers, one at 9 West 57th Street and the other at 1114 Avenue of the Americas, which have façades that slope sharply at a constantly changing, swooping angle. Both are arrogantly disrespectful of the line of buildings that marks the street, a crucial definer of the New York urban fabric, and they break this street wall in favor of a showy form that might be acceptable in a freestanding skyscraper but is difficult to justify in a dense city situation. Both buildings were designed by Gordon Bunshaft, who just a few years before, in 1967, had completed one of the most elegant and graceful glass buildings in New York, the thin-skinned Marine Midland Building at 140 Broadway. But Bunshaft's light touch seemed to have deserted him by the seventies, replaced by a rather overeager drive toward abstract curving forms that bore little relation to the architectural task at hand.

Far more pleasing, if not really more original, was Hugh Stubbins and Associates' Citicorp Center, the sleek aluminum tower completed in 1977. It was not daringly new by any means, but it did sum up the best developments of the time: it was visually smooth and cool, though here the coolness was that of a softly glowing white aluminum and not of glass; it had a street level devoted to public uses, in this case a set of stores and restaurants around an atrium; and it had a top that was sliced off at a 45-angle degree, giving the building a strong mark on the skyline. Citicorp was neither as creative urbanistically as IDS—which was the source of many of its ideas—nor as handsome sculpturally as Pennzoil or the Boston Hancock tower, but it encapsulated the best aspects of each of these buildings. Most of all, Citicorp was a sign that at the end of the 1970's there were serious changes in the expectations of even the most conservative clients as to what a skyscraper should be. It was the nature of these new expectations that was to determine the direction of skyscraper design in the 1980's.

Plaza of Citicorp Building, with St. Peter's Lutheran Church in the foreground.

Opposite: Citicorp Building, New York. Hugh Stubbins and Associates, 1977.

136

137

CHAPTER NINE

BEYOND THE BOX

By 1980, one thing was clear: the box, the rationalist dream of the International Style, was making more and more architects uncomfortable. Not only was it no longer the clean and exhilarating structure that would serve as a clarion call to a new age, but it was not even able to hold out much promise of practicality. It was generally inefficient from the standpoint of energy, and it was not as marketable from the viewpoint of real estate operators either.

For by the end of the 1970's, the success of a few notable skyscrapers of the previous decade, buildings like IDS and Pennzoil Place and Citicorp Center and John Hancock Tower, had led clients to become increasingly receptive to alternatives to the austere glass box. John Portman's projects, too, had played a role in changing public tastes—and hence market demands—toward skyscrapers that would provide occasions for social interaction, that would act as enclosed public meeting places, town squares, *agoras* of a sort, and not merely house offices or hotel rooms or identical apartment units. At the end of 1980 most of the large skyscrapers under construction in New York City contained at least some sort of public atrium, retail mall, or "galleria," as it has become common to call such places, and that alone distinguished the new group of buildings from its predecessors, Third Avenue's banal 1960's glass boxes.

And at least one building of a previous generation, the 277 Park Avenue tower by Emery Roth and Sons of 1963, was being renovated by Haines, Lundberg, Waehler to include a glass-enclosed public atrium in the space in front of the building previously occupied by an austere concrete plaza. The renovation was at the request of the building's major tenant, Chemical Bank, which insisted on (and agreed to pay for) a means by which the tower could be given public identification. The bank's recognition that 277 Park Avenue in its original form lacked such identification and its decision to try, however awkwardly, to turn the building into something resembling later skyscrapers, ranks as a final admission by the most conservative of clients that the corporate style of the 1950's no longer suited its needs.

So just as it had been economics, and not esthetics, that had ultimately won the battle of modernism after World War II, it was economics of a sort that turned builders away from the Miesian boxes with

277 Park Avenue, New York. Emery Roth and Sons, 1963; renovation 1981 by Haines, Lundberg, Waehler.

Opposite: Design for Battery Park City, New York. Cesar Pelli.

139

which they had been filling American cities since the mid-1950's. The revolution that modernism represented had been won, after all, in corporate boardrooms in the 1950's, not in European design studios in the 1920's. And the events occurring in those same boardrooms in the late 1970's and early 1980's suggest that the victory of modernism, while broad, was not particularly deep. Even Skidmore, Owings, and Merrill began to indicate doubts: in late 1980 the partners of the New York office of the firm that more than any other in the United States has been identified with the postwar corporate Miesian style invited a group of younger, so-called postmodern architects to present their work and engage in a dialogue at a private symposium. However, Skidmore consistently refused to permit the event to become a debate. It ended up with the firm's partners showing designs that they believed to be different or more eccentric than their previous work, as if to prove that they too were no longer producing Miesian buildings by reflex. And indeed, it is true—most of Skidmore, Owings, and Merrill's new work, like the Irving Trust Operations Center for lower Manhattan, to be built around an atrium, or the multi-sided tower rising at 875 Third Avenue in New York, is far from anything that the master who so inspired Skidmore could have conceived.

Irving Trust Operations Center, New York. Skidmore, Owings, and Merrill.

But the movement away from the simple application of the stark Miesian esthetic could not in itself guarantee good architecture. Many of the new Skidmore buildings already seem to possess a rote quality, as if the firm had merely discarded its old Mies model and adopted a new one, with jazzy chamfered corners and sleek atriums. That breaking with Mies could not alone provide salvation had been evident as far back as 1963, when the Pan Am Building in New York, designed by Walter Gropius, Pietro Belluschi, and Emery Roth and Sons, thrust its concrete-clad, octagonal form into the very center of overbuilt Manhattan. (Pan Am was originally to have been more Miesian and not quite as much of an urban intrusion: it was Gropius who turned the building so that it blocked Park Avenue and made it more Brutalist.) Five years later, when Edward Durell Stone and Emery Roth produced the General Motors Building in New York, where vertical piers of white marble flanked three-part projecting bay windows, rebellion resulted merely in glitz, in vulgar, showy pretension, and no more. Stone offered justifications for

141

The General Motors Building, New York. Edward Durell Stone and Emery Roth and Sons, 1968.

his design that were remarkably similar to today's expressions of dissatisfaction with Mies's modernism—but his alternative offered little that was different except surface decoration. And similarly, at a time when going beyond the International Style was more an act of rebellion than of conformity, there were an enormous number of forms produced that could at best be called curious, and were surely no more thoughtful than the simplistic International Style boxes they were replacing.

Most such buildings seemed in one way or another descendants of Pennzoil Place, the John Hancock Tower, or the Johnson and Burgee Logan towers project—glass buildings that used the modern vocabulary of materials, although they sought to arrange these materials not in a rational, straightforward way but in a freer, more sculptural, almost picturesque fashion. That is surely what Kevin Roche had done at the United Nations Plaza—a frequently seen photograph of this building from the East River, in which the United Nations Secretariat Building appears to the new tower's left and the Chrysler Building is visible to its right, makes the point. Roche's building, for all the modernity of its materials, seems to have almost as much whimsy to its form as does Chrysler. In any event, it is surely not "rationalist."

But not all of the architects of the new towers, the generation of buildings going up in the early 1980's, have quite the skill of Philip Johnson or Kevin Roche. Frequently these "late modern" towers, to use Charles Jencks's term, are forms sculpted purely for the sake of variety—a nip here, a tuck there, a setback here—and while this may go a long way toward relieving the boredom of the International Style, it seems to demonstrate nowhere near the compositional skill of the great skyscraper shapers of the 1920's. I. M. Pei, for all the finesse of his earlier skyscrapers, seemed a bit lost when he tried to vary his forms dramatically for the Texas Commerce Tower, the 70-story building that will be Houston's tallest; it is round, and full of cut-in sections and projecting sections, and one side is of granite and another of glass. The whole is rather discordant. To take another example, Eli Attia, a former associate of Philip Johnson, designed a glass tower for 101 Park Avenue at 40th Street in New York that is to be set back from its corner site on a diagonal. It will rise to 50 stories without a setback; what will enliven the form is the odd shape of the floors—they are a mix of angles yielding a final shape that appears almost to have fins. It is "unique architecture," according to an elaborate rental brochure. But the architecture, while striking and surely lively, seems not to relate particularly well to the predominantly masonry context of eclectic buildings around it, among them Grand Central Terminal. It is an object unto itself—stylish, flashy, but without either the originality and subtlety of the John Hancock Tower or the respectful modesty of the average masonry skyscraper of the 1920's.

On the other hand, there have been designs that do appear to accommodate themselves more directly to their architectural contexts. A number of glass towers designed by Kohn, Pederson, Fox are particularly noteworthy for the attention they pay to the massing, if not to the materials, of surrounding structures. Projects such as 333 Wacker Drive in Chicago and a series of schemes for the Bunker Hill area in Los Angeles are spirited and yet respectful. If they can be faulted it is for seeming almost too earnest, and too frenzied in their ins and outs, in the fashion of 101 Park Avenue. Because the Attia building, for all its claims to uniqueness, is in fact part of what has already become a genre. It has

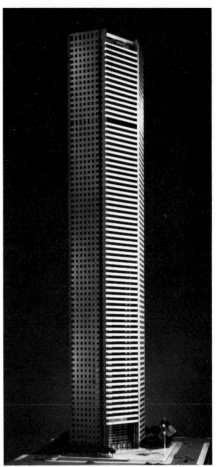

The Texas Commerce Tower, Houston. I. M. Pei.

101 Park Avenue, New York. Eli Attia.

143

been joined in its eager contortions by many other buildings.

Swanke, Hayden, and Connell's Trump Tower, the 52-story retail and apartment tower of glass for the site on Fifth Avenue once occupied by Bonwit Teller, is a further example. Here a shiny glass clashes harshly with the older masonry around it, and a series of setbacks creates a cascading effect, which while surely vibrant seems in discord with the shapes and character of the neighborhood of which it is a part. Oddly, in such a context the duller alternative, a Miesian box, might have been preferable—although the utter banality of Olympic Tower, a few blocks down Fifth Avenue, completed in 1976 to the designs of Skidmore, Owings, and Merrill, suggests that this alternative is hardly a happy one.

The design for Trump Tower seems an almost desperate attempt to put a sense of distance between the notion of the skyscraper and the notion of the box—the building has been pushed and pulled in every which way to give it form. Under its former chief designer, Der Scutt, the firm of Swanke, Hayden, Connell, and Partners became one of New York's most active commercial architects, occupying a position not unlike that of Emery Roth and Sons in the 1950's and 1960's. But whereas Emery Roth pleased developers by producing buildings that were visually simple and straightforward, even banal, Scutt has based his appeal on his ability to deliver visual excitement—to create forms that suggest

333 Wacker Drive, Chicago. Kohn, Pedersen, Fox.

Trump Tower, New York. Swanke, Hayden, Connell, and Partners.

that the architect has at last managed to triumph over the box.

Indicative of a similar impulse, though more subdued in its execution, is Edward Larrabee Barnes's IBM Building, rising at the corner of 57th Street and Madison Avenue: the structure has five sides, is 43 stories tall, and is sheathed in a gray-green granite coating. The use of masonry is welcome, as is the 4-story, greenhouselike public park that will be at the tower's base; here the new civic duty has been given noble architectural expression. This building is sleeker than a stone tower should be, but nonetheless it seems, on the whole, to be more mature, more restrained as a work of architecture than does its neighbor the Trump Tower; the box has been broken up here, but with greater discipline and dignity. Again, though, the values are those of abstraction—we are presented with pure form and not a great deal else.

The architects of the new group of sculpted towers have not, ironically, expanded their interests as much beyond those of the International Style as they might wish the public to think. They are still largely

Small public park at IBM's base.

IBM Building, New York. Edward Larrabee Barnes.

preoccupied with the effects of manipulating form; what has changed is that they have come to consider the boxes of a previous generation dull and have sought something more enlivening. There is, to be fair, generally more concern with contextual relationships, but this concern is not always primary—it often serves as an excuse for more sculpting of the box.

Also a product of the impulse toward abstraction is the effort on the part of a number of architects to vary the skin, or sheathing, of new skyscrapers. Roche himself is a leader here, with the United Nations Plaza hotel, the Worcester (County) National Bank, and other towers; so is Cesar Pelli, for some years a partner in Gruen Associates and now on his own as an architect. Pelli's design for the skin of the addition and condominium tower for the Museum of Modern Art in New York—the condominium section done in association with the office of Edward Du-

Four Leaf Towers Condominium,
Houston. Cesar Pelli.

rell Stone—is a subtle and refined assemblage of sections of glass in different tones of brown, a composition worthy of Mondrian. Yet it is not pure abstraction—it has a merit that Kevin Roche's United Nations Plaza hotel lacks, in that its exquisite skin pattern is always readable as a building; it never seems like solely a composition. The same might be said for Pelli's Four Leaf Towers Condominium proposal for Houston, in which the palette shifts to deep reds, and the glass top forms an almost conventional attic shape, intended, one presumes, to symbolize domesticity.

But the new skins, although they lack the Museum of Modern Art tower's subtlety, seem to share a quality of thinness, of tightness—they are stretched as thinly as possible across a frame, with virtually no texture, no depth, to them. The windows have no recesses as in masonry towers of old; there is a feeling that the entire structure was not so much built piece by piece as it was rolled out of a great machine. It is the absolute culmination of the machine esthetic that so fascinated

148

early modernists. Now the machine is not a great beast, but a smooth, tranquil creature. It is not really the machine esthetic but the computer esthetic, the esthetic of a postmechanical age in which objects make no noise and have no clear, visible structure to them.

Helmut Jahn, now the most prominent design partner at the Chicago firm of C. F. Murphy, has produced a number of provocative buildings, which, like Roche's, Barnes's, Pei's, and Pelli's, seem cleverly to exploit the virtues of abstraction. Jahn's new designs, with the exception of the cool and clean Xerox Center just completed in Chicago—a handsome example of the computer esthetic, and a visually cheerful presence in the downtown Loop—have managed to combine the modernist tendency toward abstraction with some very real and overt imagery. Jahn's proposed Northwest Terminal Project for Chicago has at its top cascading mountains of glass, tumbling like a waterfall; his One South Wacker building in Chicago is a 40-story setback structure with an ornamental pattern in

Xerox Center, Chicago. Helmut Jahn, 1980.

the glass skin and an elaborate top; his proposed addition to the Chicago Board of Trade is an almost exact reproduction in glass of the original Board of Trade's 1930's setback massing and pyramidal top.

Jahn's work calls to mind that of the most energetic, and surely most debated, skyscraper designer of our time, Philip Johnson. With his partner John Burgee, Johnson has produced a series of designs that have challenged even the most current notions of what skyscrapers should be. Despite his successes with IDS in setting the trend toward the social skyscraper and with Pennzoil in setting the trend toward the abstract one, Johnson has rejected these movements, even as they continue to grow, in favor of what can best be called a quest into the history of the tower form. His new skyscrapers are not so much sculptural as they are pictorial—they are collections of images from towers of the past, reconstituted in modern materials, with modern innards, for modern pur-

One South Wacker, Chicago. Helmut Jahn.

The Chicago Board of Trade Addition.
Helmut Jahn.

The Chicago Board of Trade. Holabird and Root, 1930.

*The American Telephone and
Telegraph Building, New York.
Johnson and Burgee.*

*Detail of rear entrance of the
AT&T Building.*

poses. His most blatantly historical designs, and surely his most famous, are the projects for the American Telephone and Telegraph Company headquarters in New York and the PPG Industries Headquarters in Pittsburgh. Both are now under construction.

The A.T.&T. Building has the distinction of being among the most controversial buildings of the age. It is a 37-story tower of pinkish granite, rising to the unusual height for a structure of so few stories of 500 feet, with an immense broken pediment at the top and a series of Renaissance-inspired arches at the base. The midsection is a fairly routine vertical shaft, though Johnson likes to say that its source was Raymond Hood. The building so startled the editors of the *New York Times* that they put a rendering of it on the front page when the design was made public in 1978; the public dialogue that followed, though fairly critical of the scheme, was remarkable for the degree of interest it caused. It seemed as if everyone, layman and architect alike, felt moved to speak. "Idiosyncratic. Self-indulgent. Frivolous. . . . This preposterous design is perhaps a logical denouement for decades of increasingly mannered historicism," said James Marston Fitch, the historian. "If Mies van der Rohe were alive today, he would regard this design with nothing less than loathing," wrote Paul Gapp in the Chicago *Tribune*.

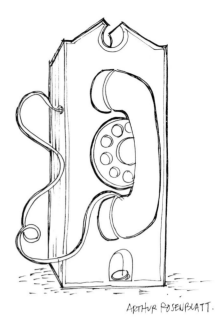

A cartoon of proposed AT&T design by Arthur Rosenblatt.

The discussion seemed characterized by an air of shock, as if the public—not to mention the architectural profession—was unable to conceive of this design as a serious plan for a building. Ironically, there is much about A.T.&T. that is conventional; for example, it is the only major skyscraper of the current generation in New York that will have floor plans of standard rectangular shape, instead of parallelograms or polygons. But the public perception of this building as bizarre was hardly without foundation—A.T.&T.'s top has frequently been compared to a Chippendale highboy, and, indeed, it is difficult not to see the comparison. The building does look like a piece of furniture or an object blown up from a smaller scale, and it calls to mind Hans Hollein's photomontage of a Rolls-Royce grille set against the skyline of Manhattan. The public outcry over A.T.&T. was based on the assumption, however, that the unusual pedimented top would be clearly visible, and that the building could be perceived as a single, unified object. That seems unlikely to be the case: A.T.&T. is on a tight city street (too tight, indeed, and too dense, as it builds itself up more and more heavily), and unless several surrounding blocks are demolished, the top will be barely visible from the street. It will be seen best from other buildings.

This top may still appear startling, even grotesque, when viewed from neighboring towers, of course, but the bottom may well appear noble. Its scale and details suggest the possibility of a kind of civic grandeur seen in no private commercial building in half a century. And Johnson and Burgee were correct in realizing that the parts of a building may well serve different masters: the bottom serves the street and the top serves the skyline, and they need not appear to be a fully unified object.

But they do require a certain coherence, a certain sense of appropriateness together, as well as good proportions, and here is where A.T.&T. seems most likely to fall short. There is a feeling of awkwardness to this building, a feeling that the parts of it have little in common. It is not the unified object that such eclectic works of the 1920's as the Standard Oil Building or the American Radiator Building were—despite the fact that it emerges out of a desire to join in their tradition, out

153

Maiden Lane Tower, New York. Johnson and Burgee.

of a recognition that the essential quality of the New York skyline has always been a kind of theatricality, a flamboyance based on a reinterpretation of historic form.

There is more unity, but also more theatricality, in the PPG building. Logically for the headquarters of a glass manufacturer, it is sheathed in glass, but instead of the abstraction of most recent glass towers, there is almost pure historicism. It is to be a Gothic tower, not unlike the tower of the Houses of Parliament in Westminster, rendered in glass. This time there has been no attempt to justify the unusual form in terms of the architectural traditions of the city of which it will be a part—this one is expected to stand on its own, with only the rationale, perhaps, that a tower that looked good in stone to the nineteenth century ought surely to look good in glass to the twentieth.

Time will tell. But as much as the recognition behind both of these designs that skyscrapers belong to the art of composition and the art of symbol making is welcome, it is difficult to be certain in either case that the design will come off. The romanticism is too sentimental, too easy—architecture made by Tchaikovsky. Similar things might be said about Johnson and Burgee's new tower for Maiden Lane in New York, which attempts to replicate in brick the castellated motifs of the great Federal Reserve Bank by York and Sawyer next door. The romanticism is welcome: the Palazzo Strozzi imitation that is the Federal Reserve is worthy of respect, but it is uncertain whether the Johnson building will come off as respectful architecture or weak pictorialism.

It is easier to be sympathetic with the less literal approach to romantic classicism taken by Ulrich Franzen, whose new Philip Morris Headquarters in New York tries hard to interpret classical forms in a way that

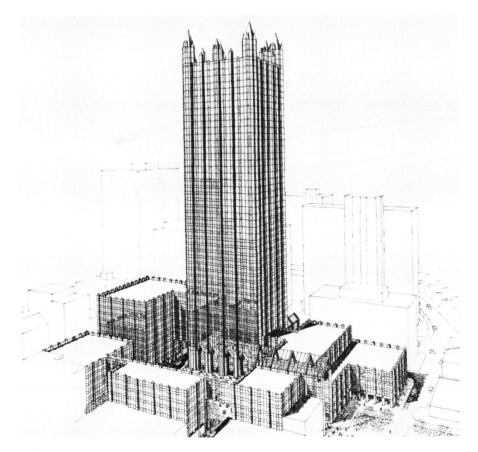

Pittsburgh Plate Glass Industries Headquarters, Pittsburgh. Johnson and Burgee.

154

Philip Morris Headquarters, New York. Ulrich Franzen.

relates closely to the demands of its context. But it is not a particularly graceful building, and it treats the notion of respect for surroundings with such exaggeration that it indulges in the absurdity of different façade treatments for the two main streets it faces. Still, it is a deeply earnest building, a quality that, if it was absent in skyscraper design a few years ago, has surely now returned in vast supply.

Johnson and Burgee's other efforts range from a rather conventionally sculpted round tower in San Francisco, chopped up with a number of faceted sides in the manner that IDS made fashionable, to the Republic Bank Center in Houston, which contains three setback tower sections in glass, mounting sumptuously toward the top in a profile reminiscent of the most romantic expressionist skyline views of the 1930's. And

155

Transco, Houston. Johnson and Burgee.

The Panhellenic Hotel (now the Beekman Tower Hotel), New York. John Mead Howells, 1928.

156

as if this were not enough, for its base Johnson and Burgee plan a huge masonry banking wing that seems a cross between Richardson and Ledoux—huge arches and a gabled roof, an ancient monument created brand new to serve as an entrance to a contemporary tower that alludes to the 1930's. It will surely be impressive, but it is hard not to feel here, as elsewhere, that the architects have been so eager to let us sample their historical wares that they have given them all to us in a single building.

Far more coherent, and the most promising of all of Johnson and Burgee's new efforts, is another Houston tower, this one grander still—a freestanding tower of glass, called Transco, in which the four corners are progressively cut away and set back to reveal a splendid profile. Johnson admits influences from Sir Edwin Lutyens and Bertram Goodhue here, and it is hard not to think of the Panhellenic Hotel, which sits just outside the architect's office window in the Seagram Building. However, his building is not an imitation of these buildings, and it is not a pastiche of parts of others. It is a complete integration of works of the past into a fresh and clear whole—a work that seems clearly to be a skyscraper, that throws no confusing signals at us as A.T.&T. does, and yet a work that expands our view of what skyscrapers can be. It is a tower that speaks of height, yet seems firmly implanted on the ground; it is a design that has both liveliness and dignity to it. It is a design that seems to have learned from the past, and to have carried that knowledge somewhere one could not have imagined going before. It is hard not to look at this tower and think again of Root, Sullivan, Goodhue, and Hood; none of them could have designed Transco, yet their works seem oddly in accord with it.

Whatever the merits of the designs this period is producing, it seems certain that the architects active right now have brought a degree of inventiveness to skyscraper design that has as its only true peer the work of the 1920's. In each period there has been a tendency to exploit history, often rather arbitrarily, and in each period the art of composition has played a crucial role in the process of design. Each time has been preoccupied with finding means of enlivening the average building's effect on the cityscape. In other words, the creation of an architecture of visual stimulation has been a priority for both eras. In this sense the spirit of New York seems to have prevailed over that of Chicago. The skyscraper tradition of New York, the preference for the picturesque and the flamboyant over the rational, seems certainly to have become a characteristic of the 1980's in all places.

Yet the skyscrapers of the 1980's are obviously not like those of the 1920's, and they are not likely to become so. Vast technological differences aside, the buildings of the current generation seem in comparison to their predecessors not a little strained and awkward; they rarely possess the grace and assurance of the Tribune Tower or the American Radiator Building, not to mention that monument of the decade before, the Woolworth Building. One senses today that history is being used not as part of the art of composing a tower, but almost in opposition to it, as in A.T.&T., where the historical elements seem out of kilter with the building's mass. With its oblong form A.T.&T. tries to be a sleeker box than it is, and though the historical references themselves are pleasing, the scale and combinations Johnson and Burgee have given them create a sense of discord. Is this the deliberate shock of the new, or is it merely the routine awkwardness of poor composition?

Republic Bank Center, Houston. Johnson and Burgee.

Johnson and Burgee appear likely to do so much better with Transco that it is perhaps not entirely fair to dwell on A.T.&T., a building that for all its compositional flaws will clearly be a deeply powerful, perhaps even a moving, urban presence. And A.T.&T., if for nothing else must be appreciated for its status as the first major postmodern monument to catch the public eye. Yet it is hard not to feel a certain dislocation in many other architects' work today, a sense that the historical elements being used are not fully in accord with everything else going on. They seem to have emerged out of an almost desperate desire to find alternatives to the boredom of Miesian towers, and they do not always suggest a particular coherence. One feels more unity, if not profundity, in the computer-esthetic towers of Roche and Pei and Pelli and Jahn—here, though the imagery may be disturbing, it seems most emphatically to yield objects that speak with self-assurance.

These two strains—the historicist and computer esthetics—may yet join. There are hints of a connection in Transco, as well as in such projects as Jahn's Chicago Board of Trade Addition; it can also be felt in the Zimmer, Gunsul, Frasca Partnership's Fountain Plaza Project for Portland, Oregon, a tower of modern materials given a heavy base and a pyramidal top. In profile it is like Warren and Wetmore's Heckscher Building of 1925 on Fifth Avenue in New York, rendered cool and sleek. None of these buildings is yet complete, and it is always dangerous to

Fountain Plaza Project, Portland, Oregon. Zimmer, Gunsul, Frasca Partnership.

predict too much on the basis of models and drawings, but each of these designs does seem to emerge from a set of ideas that, while complex, come together to create a coherent and unified whole.

Perhaps the finest design yet produced in this genre, and as strong a testament to the potential of merging the historicist and computer esthetics as one could ask for, is Cesar Pelli's scheme for Battery Park City in lower Manhattan. The project is vast—it will include six million square feet of office space—and Pelli has proposed four bulky towers of glass and granite, with frequent setbacks and low pyramidal or domed tops. The buildings will be largely of granite on their lower floors, and at each setback will take on more glass surface, literally symbolizing a move away from historicism and toward abstraction as they rise. Most encouraging is the strong relationship these buildings will have not only to the physical form of their surroundings—there will be carefully preserved visual axes so as not to block river views from neighboring buildings, for example—but also to the tradition of New York building. The setbacks, the masonry, the decorated tops of the greatest of New York towers are echoed here; since neither Transco nor the Board of Trade Addition will be built in New York, this complex seems destined to become the major keeper of the New York skyscraper tradition in our time.

Battery Park City, New York.
Cesar Pelli.

159

Significantly, it was the closeness of this design to the traditional New York skyscraper—the "New Yorkness" of it—that led Battery Park City's developer, Olympia and York, to select Pelli's scheme over the five competitors in a small, invited architectural competition that the real estate firm held in 1980. The competition was not an event of the scope of the Chicago Tribune competition, but it offered a significant look at the state of the art as practiced by several firms which have come to assume active roles in the continued evolution of skyscraper design: Edward Larabee Barnes, architect of IBM; Mitchell/Giurgola, a sensitive and innovative firm whose Penn Mutual skyscraper in Philadelphia, of 1976, is a particularly thoughtful juxtaposition of a new tower beside an older skyscraper; Hellmuth, Obata, and Kassabaum, an immense commercial firm; Kohn, Pederson, Fox, whose skyscrapers have shown increasing promise; Davis, Brody, a firm known best for its housing; and Zimmer, Gunsul, Frasca, the architects of Fountain Plaza Project in Portland.

Oddly, only Pelli sought to work literally within the traditions of the New York setback skyscraper of the 1920's and 1930's, though he interpreted those traditions largely in glass. No architect offered a plain box—in 1980, they would sooner have turned in their professional licenses—but the other competitors tended either to fairly restrained, almost dull towers, or to rather outlandish schemes. Barnes produced dignified buildings in the style of IBM, with diagonal slices here and there;

The Kohn, Pedersen, Fox entry in the Battery Park City competition.

The Mitchell/Giurgola entry in the Battery Park City competition.

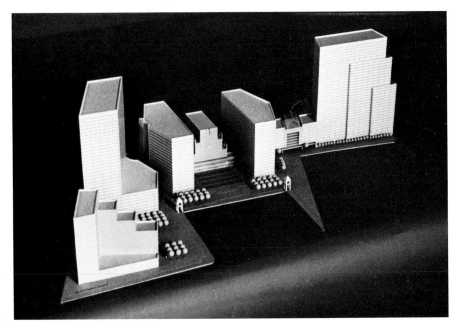

Rendering of a gallery in the Battery Park City complex.

while Hellmuth, Obata, and Kassabaum came up with a set of glittering towers full of simplistic setbacks at the top. Kohn, Pederson, Fox proposed four identical towers, each with a rounded façade facing southwest. Mitchell/Giurgola seemed to understand the site best, but its buildings were dull. In the end only Pelli's scheme seemed both lively in itself and appropriate to this crucial site.

But even the quality of such designs as Battery Park City, Transco, and the Board of Trade Addition does not mean that every attempt to join the strains of the historicist and the computer esthetics will meet with success. Less pleasing, but surely startling, is the planned Hercules Inc. headquarters for Wilmington, Delaware, by Kohn, Pederson, Fox. Here a massive structure, wider than it is high, has been given a masonry base and a glass upper section; the whole looks for all the world like a remnant of a nineteenth-century commercial building upon which has been plopped a cool, computer-esthetic top. In this building the two instincts of our time have not so much merged as been forced into collision, and the result is a bizarre mix of historicist yearnings and modernist leanings, all unresolved.

As shocking visually, though more subtle in its ideas, is Michael Graves's design for the Portland Public Services Building, now under construction. Graves won the commission in competition, thanks to a jury headed by Philip Johnson; together with Fountain Plaza this struc-

161

ture should make Portland a mecca for students of developing trends in skyscraper design. The Graves building looks like nothing else in the history of tall buildings, though its ideological leanings are toward Johnson's historicist school. It is heavy and boxy, shaped almost like a cube, and its exterior is a mix of vast, overscaled classical elements and simple, punched-in windows. The stucco façade is polychromed in shades of rust and orange and gray, and the overall sense is of classical elements out of context—placed almost in a cubist mode of composition. If this building resembles any extant structures, they are the unusual high-rise warehouses that were built in Manhattan in the 1920's and 1930's; it has the same surprising mix of starkness and tacked-on detail. Yet it is powerful indeed—if there is any building of our time that appears to speak with fresh conviction, with a firm self-assurance, it is this one.

Graves's building, no less than the Kohn, Pederson, Fox Hercules design, articulates the dilemma facing the architect of the tall, or even moderately high, building today. How to make a coherent design when the basic impulses behind the building—the need to relate to context, the desire to relate to history, and the demands of high-rise technology— do not seem at all consistent with each other? Moreover, how to make a coherent design when the act of expressing a new technology, not to mention the very fact of building tall, is no longer meaningful? The Portland and Wilmington buildings are not very tall by the standards of the twentieth century, though they would both be immense by the standards of the nineteenth. In any case it is no longer an event to create a building of great height. The tallest buildings of our time, ironically, like the World Trade Center, have often been the most banal—all they have had to offer was a quality that could no longer ignite the architectural imagination. And technology seems only slightly more able to provide an impetus to creativity. Most new skyscrapers that have been a direct expression of technological prowess, buildings like Yamasaki's Rainier Bank of Seattle, or Gunnar Birkets's Federal Reserve Bank of Minneapolis, which is slung from piers like a suspension bridge, have seemed exhibitionistic and strained. Only the sleek computer esthetic appears able to convince as a technological expression today—and it is more symbol

Hercules, Inc., Headquarters, Wilmington, Delaware, Kohn, Pedersen, Fox.

162

Portland Public Services Building, Portland, Oregon. Michael Graves.

of the romance of technology than it is a literal expression of the actual technology of building.

So there is a quality of romanticism that ties all of the new skyscrapers of our time together, from Graves to Johnson to Pelli to Roche. Different buildings all, and different kinds of romanticism, yet in each case the romantic impulse is turned away from its manifestations in earlier skyscrapers. No longer is it height that is expressed—in fact, Graves's building tries rather hard to look squat. Nothing could be further from Sullivan's exhortation that the skyscraper be "tall, every inch of it tall." The Portland building is a great decorated box; it will have considerable power, but it is surely not Sullivan's "proud and soaring thing."

Similarly, the notion of expressing structure has lost its impact. It is no longer convincing: Skidmore, Owings, and Merrill may have excited Chicago with the great X-braces marching up the John Hancock Center's 95-story façade, but when Hugh Stubbins chose to hide the similar X-braces of his Citicorp Center behind its metal skin, there were no cries of foul; no one felt that Stubbins had been dishonest. The visually pleasanter form that resulted was justification enough for this act in the late 1970's. And of course structure is entirely concealed in the cool buildings of the computer esthetic, which do not even reveal floor divisions. They romanticize the idea of postmechanical technology, which is an altogether different matter than displaying the mechanical technology by which they were built.

163

There is a temptation to dismiss much of what is going on now as not only romantic but effete—games, sometimes rather precious ones, being played by architects who no longer have any real innovating left to do. The skyscraper has not only been invented, it has grown and developed from its strong theoretical beginnings through modernist rationalism and then back to the present preoccupation with the composing of architectural form for its own sake, apart from the demands and requirements of physical construction.

But one can just as easily look at this moment in architectural history as a baroque flowering. The problems of the early skyscrapers have been solved—we know how to make buildings that express great height. So we turn toward the integration of more conventional architectural concerns with skyscraper design, and toward the elaboration of skyscraper form that follows from it. This seems, of course, like what the architects of the first two decades of this century were doing, but it was not precisely the same. Their eclectic skyscrapers were attempts to integrate modern technology directly into nineteenth-century historicist traditions; they were not postmodern esthetic statements but premodern ones, buildings that were born of a certain innocence common to all American eclectic architecture of the first decades of this century.

There is no such innocence today: architects now, even those who reject it, have tasted of modernism, and its effects are felt throughout everything now designed. This is a time much more like the Baroque—a time of intricate and ironic visual tricks, exuberance, and self-indulgence. It is a time of excess, but it is also a time of promise.

Drawing of the Portland Public Services Building from the park side.

Opposite: Composite of buildings under construction in midtown Manhattan, 1980.

NOTES

CHAPTER ONE

Page 5, "Washington Monument": "Tallest Skyscraper to Stand on Broadway," New York Times, Feb. 22, 1906.

Page 7, "Singer Tower": Ibid.

Page 8, Promotional piece: W. Parker Chase, *New York: The Wonder City* (New York: Wonder City Publishing Co., 1932), p. 181.

Page 8, "World": Rem Koolhaas, *Delirious New York* (New York: Oxford University Press, 1978), p. 68. Koolhaas correctly points out that the true Manhattan skyscraper was born after the turn of the century, not before.

Page 8, "Construction here": "Singer Tower Soon to Be in Second Place," *New York Times,* Dec. 29, 1907.

Page 8, "Something larger": Quoted in Koolhaas, from New York *Herald,* May 13, 1906.

Page 10, "Height of buildings": Montgomery Schuyler, "To Curb the Skyscraper," *Architectural Record,* Oct. 1908.

Pages 10–11, "Great outrage": Ibid.

Page 11, "Structure": "Skyscrapers Bad for City," *New York Times,* July 3, 1908.

Page 12, Tax on skyscrapers: "Would Colonize the Skyscrapers," *New York Times,* Aug. 7, 1908.

Pages 12–13, "Assert themselves": David Knickerbocker Boyd, "The Skyscraper and the Street," *American Architecture and Building News,* Nov. 18, 1908.

Page 13, Ventilation: Post's and Burnham's remarks were made at a symposium on the question of height limitations for skyscrapers sponsored by the Architectural League of New York on April 4, 1894. The session, which also included remarks by Dankmar Adler, Louis Sullivan's partner, was a precursor of the debate to follow after the turn of the century. Post, one of New York's most eminent architects, was an early and ardent opponent of unlimited skyscraper construction.

Page 13, "Oppressive and absurd": "Tall Buildings," *New York Times,* Aug. 13, 1906.

Page 15, Build the park themselves: Louis I. Horowitz, *The Towers of New York* (New York: Simon and Schuster, 1937), pp. 153–54.

Page 15, "Giants of the market": Henry James, *The American Scene* (New York: Charles Scribner's Sons, 1907), p. 75.

CHAPTER TWO

Page 17, "Monotony": Thomas Hastings, "High Buildings and Good Architecture: What Principles Should Govern Their Design," *American Architecture and Building News,* Nov. 17, 1894. Text of paper delivered at American Institute of Architects Convention, Oct. 1894.

Page 17, "The Tall Office Building": Published originally in *Lippincott's,* March 1896; reproduced frequently, including in Louis Sullivan, *Kindergarten Chats and Other Writings* (New York: George Wittenborn, 1947).

Page 19, Natural forms: William Jordy provides a lucid explanation of Sullivan's intent as a maker of ornament in *American Buildings and Their Architects* (New York: Doubleday, 1972), vol. 3, which offers a sound introduction to Sullivan's work in general. Sullivan's ornament has been discussed, at least briefly, by virtually every historian who has given attention to the architect's work, with varying degrees of acceptance: International Style modernists frequently rejected it as insufficiently pure. Sullivan himself prepared a book entitled *A System of Architectural Ornament* in 1922, which was published posthumously in 1924.

Page 20, "Spring into life": Sullivan, *Kindergarten Chats,* pp. 28–30.

Page 21, "National style": "A Great Architectural Problem," *Inland Architect and News Record,* June 1890, p. 68.

Page 23, Dramatic shift: Winston Weisman, "A New View of Skyscraper History"—in his *Rise of a New American Architecture* (New York: Praeger, 1968), p. 119—calls Equitable the first skyscraper on the basis of the ability it demonstrated to make height economically desirable by means of the elevator.

Page 26, "Audacity": William Archer, *America To-day,* 1900, cited in Jordy, *American Buildings and Their Architects,* p. 45.

Page 34, "Venetian blinds": Vincent Scully, *American Architecture and Urbanism* (New York: Praeger, 1969), p. 110.

CHAPTER THREE

Page 38, "Unconscious absorption": New York Times, March 10, 1908.

Page 39, "Metropolitan Life Tower": "The Singer Tower Soon to Be in Second Place," *New York Times,* Dec. 29, 1907.

Page 39, "Never realized": Both towers are shown in Weisman, "A New View of Skyscraper History," in *The Rise of an American Architecture,* p. 145.

Page 44, "Parisianized architecture": Montgomery Schuyler, "The Towers of Manhattan, and Notes on the Woolworth Building," *Architectural Record,* Feb. 1913.

Page 44, "Higher it mounts": Quoted in Francisco Mujica, *History of the Sky-scraper* (New York: Da Capo Press, 1977, reprint of 1929 edition), p. 34.

Pages 44–45, "To obtain it": The Cathedral of Commerce (New York: Broadway-Park Place Company, 1917).

CHAPTER FOUR

Page 49, "Epoch making": Henry-Russell Hitchcock, *In the Nature of Materials* (New York: Da Capo Press, 1975 reprint of original 1942 edition).

Pages 50–51, "New problems": Ludwig Mies van der Rohe, "Two Glass Skyscrapers," from *Fruhlicht,* 1:122–24, 1922. Reprinted in Philip Johnson, *Mies van der Rohe* (New York: Museum of Modern Art, 1947 and 1978), p. 187.

Page 51, "Glass surfaces": Ibid.

Page 53, "Joy of life": Sullivan wrote his comments in the *Architectural Record,* and they were reprinted in the book published by the *Tribune* as a record of the competition.

Page 53, Manfredo Tafuri: "The Disenchanted Mountain," in Manfredo Tafuri and Georgio Ciucci, *The American City* (Cambridge: MIT Press, 1979), p. 402.

Pages 58–59, "Born old": Lewis Mumford, "The Search for Something More," published in 1928. Reprinted in *Architecture as a Home for Man* (New York: Architectural Record Books, 1975).

Page 59, "Design": Ibid.

Page 59, "Modern feeling": Ibid.

Page 59, "Something more": Ibid.

Page 59, "Strawberry festival": Ibid.

Page 63, "Everything else": Raymond M. Hood, "Exterior Architecture of Office Buildings," *Architectural Forum,* Sept. 1924, p. 97.

Page 65, "Great": Fred B. Humphrey to W. E. Hardy, July 7, 1920. Nebraska State Historical Society, quoted in Henry-Russell Hitchcock and William Seale, *Temples of Democracy* (New York: Harcourt Brace, 1976).

CHAPTER FIVE

Page 86, "Disappear altogether": "At 132 Stories Income Disappeared," *American Architect,* Dec. 1929, p. 30.

Page 88, "Stop traffic": Literary Digest, Dec. 11, 1926, p. 12.

Page 88, "Municipality": Thomas Hastings, "The City of Dreadful Height," *Forum,* April, 1927.

Page 88, "In the air": Ibid.

Pages 88–89, London's traffic problems: "Skyscraper and Traffic," *Literary Digest,* March 5, 1927, p. 21.

Page 89, "Skyscrapers of New York": Le Corbusier, *When the Cathedrals Were White* (New York: McGraw-Hill, new ed., 1964), p. 55.

Pages 90–91, "Congestion is good": Quoted in Henry N. Wright's "The Case for the Skyscraper," *Architectural Forum,* Dec. 1939.

Page 91, "Comprehension": W. Parker Chase, *New York: The Wonder City* (New York: Wonder City Publishing Co., 1932), p. 3.

CHAPTER SIX

Page 94, "Proto-jukebox": Vincent Scully, *American Architecture and Urbanism* (New York: Praeger, 1969), p. 154.

Page 94, "Steel cage": Henry-Russell Hitchcock and Philip Johnson, *The International Style* (New York: W. W. Norton and Co., new ed., 1966), p. 43.

Page 97, "International Style": Robert A. M. Stern, *George Howe: Toward a Modern American Architecture* (New Haven Conn.: Yale University Press, 1974), p. 117.

Page 99, Retrogressive: Alan Balfour, *Rockefeller Center: Architecture as Theater* (New York: McGraw-Hill, 1978) p. 39.

CHAPTER SEVEN

Pages 105–6, United Nations Organization: Lewis Mumford, "Buildings as Symbols," reprinted in *From the Ground Up* (New York: Harcourt Brace and World, 1956), published originally in *The New Yorker,* 1947.

Page 112 "All the more beauty": Phyllis Lambert, "How a Building Gets Built, *Vassar Alumnae Magazine,* Feb. 1959.

CHAPTER NINE

Page 153, James Marston Fitch: "The Livable City," Municipal Arts Society, New York, July 1978

Page 153, Paul Gapp: "The Livable City," July 1978.

INDEX

PHOTOGRAPH SOURCES

177

Kohn Pedersen Fox (pages 144, 160 above, 162)

Larry Kutnicki (page 94 left, 106 left)

The Landmark Society of Western New York, Rochester, N.Y. (70 Pine Street in New York, color section)

Courtesy, Library of Congress, Prints and Photographs Division (pages 7 left, 25, 27, 40 left, 41, 54, 56, 66, 156 left)

Nathaniel Lieberman (page 165); © 1972 (IDS Building, color section)

J. P. Lohman Co. (Chrysler Building Lobby Elevators, color section)

Long Island Historical Society (page 67)

Metropolitan Museum of Art, Gift of Alfred Steiglitz, 1933 (page 38 above)

Mitchell / Giurgola (page 160 below)

Movie Star News (page 85 below)

C. F. Murphy (page 131)

Museum of Modern Art (page 17)

Museum of the City of New York (pages 5, 7 right, 9, 11, 14, 36, 39 left, 40 right, 43, 55, 59 above, 68, 75, 78 right, 92, 95, 106)

Naramore Bain Brady and Johanson (page 129)

Nebraska Art Association, Courtesy of Sheldon Memorial Art Gallery, University of Nebraska, Lincoln ("Shelton at Night," color section)

Nebraska State Historical Society (page 64)

New-York Historical Society (pages 2, 13)

Newspaper Collection, The New York Public Library, Astor, Lenox and Tilden Foundations (page 10)

New York Telephone Company (page 57 right)

The Ohio Historical Society, Inc. (page 65)

Olympia and York (pages 138, 159, 161)

Otis Elevator Company (pages 12, 15)

I. M. Pei & Partners, Architects (pages 118, 119, 143 right)

Cesar Pelli & Associates (pages 147, 148, 159, 161)

Philadelphia Saving Fund Society (page 96)

Port Authority of New York and New Jersey (page 128 below)

John Portman Associates (pages 120 below, 121)

Price Tower (page 110)

Max Protetch Gallery, New York City (Portland Public Office Building, park facade, color section)

© Cervin Robinson (pages 57 left, 62, 70 right, 76, 78 left)

Roche and Dinkeloo and Associates (pages 116, 117)

Rockefeller Center, Inc. (pages 85 above, 86, 98, 99, 100, 101, 115)

© Arthur Rosenblatt (page 153)

Emery Roth and Sons (pages 69 left, 104 right, 128 above, 141 left)

David Sagarin (page 42)

From the Collection of Leah Schnall (pages 38 below, Flatiron Building and Metropolitan Life Tower, color section)

Courtesy, The Singer Company (page 6)

Skidmore, Owings, and Merrill (pages 107, 133, 140)

Malcolm Smith / Jane Doggett (page 102)

Ezra Stoller/© Esto (pages 105 below, 107, 111, 112, 113, 133)

Hugh Stubbins and Associates (pages 136 right, 137)

Swanke, Hayden, Connell and Partners (page 145)

Transamerica Corporation (page 130 left)

2 Park Avenue Associates (lobby of 2 Park Avenue, color section)

United Nations (page 105 above)

U.S. Realty Investments (page 73 above)

Western Reserve Historical Society (page 73 below)

F. W. Woolworth Co. (pages 45, 47)

Frank Lloyd Wright Memorial Foundation (page 49)

The Wrigley Company (page 53)

Wurts Bros.-Photo (page 32, 60 right, 61, 71, 74, 81, 84, 97)

Zimmer, Gunsul, Frasca Partnership (page 158)

In some cases photographs are owned or were provided by someone other than the photographer. The photographers of those photographs, where known, are given below.

Berenice Abbott (page 95)

Paul Beswick (page 120 below)

Karl Bischoff (page 129)

Robert Bischoff (page 57 right)

Louis Checkman (page 124 below, 146)

Kenneth Champlin (pages 138, 147, 148, 159, 161)

George Cserna (page 118 right)

Alexander Georges (page 121)

Gorchev and Gorchev (page 119)

Jack Horner (page 162)

J. A. McAlonen III (page 158)

Norman McGrath (page 136 right, Chrysler Building lobby elevators, color section)

Richard Nickel (pages 16, 108)

John Orfield (page 160 below)

Richard Payne (pages 123, 125, 126 right)

James R. Steinkamp (pages 150, 151 left)

Studio 350, Inc. (page 120 above)

Underhill (pages 36, 41, 43, 55, 92, 156 left)

Nick Wheeler (page 137 left)

Wurts Bros.-Photo (pages 69, 75)

The text of this book was film set in Fairfield, the first type face from the hand of the distinguished American artist and engraver Rudolph Ruzicka. In its structure Fairfield displays the sober and sane qualities of a master craftsman whose talent has long been dedicated to clarity. It is this trait that accounts for the trim grace and virility, the spirited design and sensitive balance of this original type face.

Rudolph Ruzicka was born in Bohemia in 1883 and came to America in 1894. He designed and illustrated many books and created a considerable list of individual prints—wood engravings, line engravings on copper, aquatints.

This book was composed by The Clarinda Company, Clarinda, Iowa. The four-color separations for the insert were done by Coral Color, Amityville, New York. The book was printed and bound by The Murray Printing Company, Westford, Massachusetts.

Typography and binding design by Whitehouse and Katz, New York.